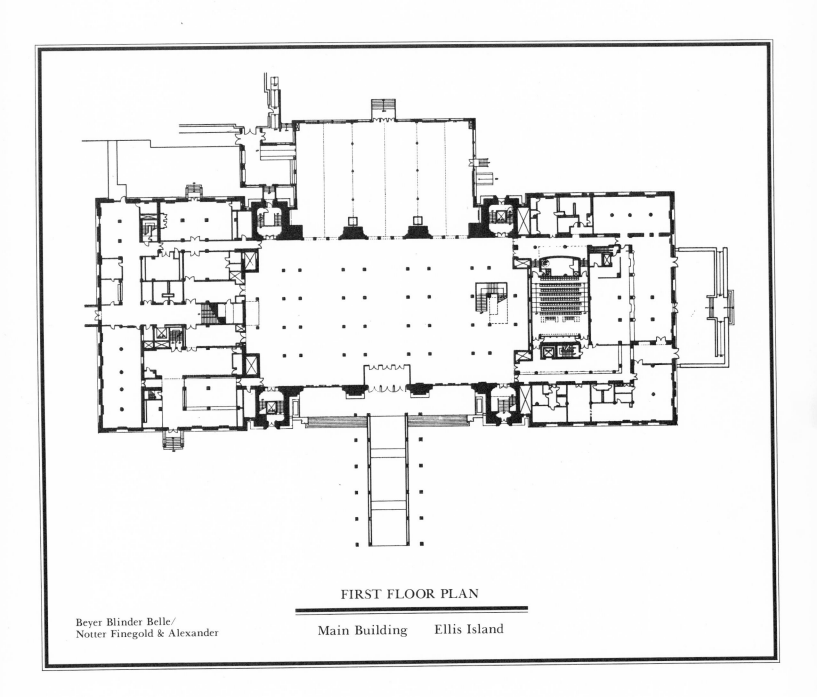

FIRST FLOOR PLAN

Beyer Blinder Belle/
Notter Finegold & Alexander

Main Building   Ellis Island

ELLIS ISLAND

"The word 'America' in those days was the wish, the dream, and the hope of every person. We called that the Golden Land. It was the desire of every human being to reach the gates of the Golden Land."
—Gertrude Yellin, emigrated from Russia in 1921

ELLIS ISLAND

Wilton S. Tifft
Foreword by Lee Iacocca

OFFICIAL LICENSEE

ELLIS ISLAND
1892–1992

TM © 1987 SL/EIF, INC

CB

CONTEMPORARY
BOOKS

CHICAGO

Library of Congress Cataloging-in-Publication Data

Tifft, Wilton.
    Ellis Island / Wilton S. Tifft.
        p.   cm.
    Includes bibliographical references.
    ISBN 0-8092-4418-7
    1. Ellis Island Immigration Station (New York,
N.Y.)—History.
    2. United States—Emigration and immigration—
History.   3. United States—Emigration and
immigration—Government policy—History.
    I. Title.
    JV6483.T53   1990
    325′.1′0973—dc20   89-22352
                           CIP

Blueprints on end papers: © 1989 Beyer Blinder Belle/
Notter Finegold & Alexander Associated Architects.
Reprinted by permission.

Illustration on page viii by Rosemary Morrissey-Herzberg

Photos on pages 86, 89, 232, 237, and 239 courtesy of
the National Park Service.

Photo on page 179: © 1989 Wilton S. Tifft

Book design by William Ewing, Ewing/Davison Design
Group, Inc., Northbrook, Illinois

Copyright © 1990 by Wilton S. Tifft
All rights reserved
Published by Contemporary Books, Inc.
180 North Michigan Avenue, Chicago, Illinois 60601
Manufactured in the United States of America
International Standard Book Number: 0-8092-4418-7

This book is dedicated to my parents,
Bela and Ellen Tifft

and
in memory of two friends,
Jack Anderson
and
Shirley C. Burden.

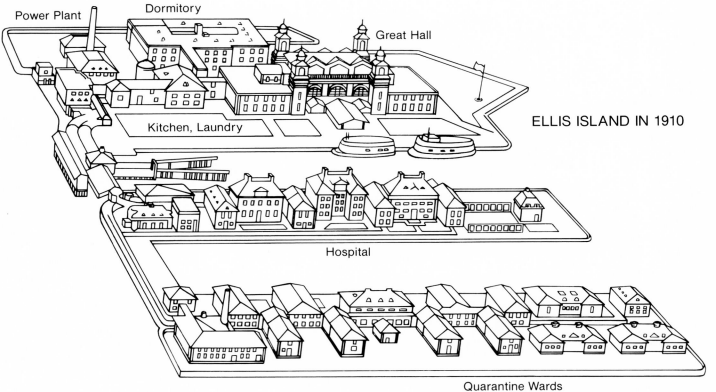

Power Plant

Dormitory

Great Hall

Kitchen, Laundry

ELLIS ISLAND IN 1910

Hospital

Quarantine Wards

Contents

Foreword

Ellis Island holds great personal meaning for me. It was here that my own parents, Nicola and Antoinette Iacocca, first set foot on American soil. My father came alone in 1902 at the age of twelve from San Marco, a little village twenty-five miles northeast of Naples.

I often wonder what he must have felt when he sailed past the Statue of Liberty on his way to Ellis Island. Fear? Excitement? Anxiety? And as I look at the photographs in this book, I realize that he must have felt all of these and more. Like so many others, he arrived in this country with little more than the clothes on his back and a heart full of hope.

My father settled in Allentown, Pennsylvania. He worked hard taking on odd jobs, mostly as an apprentice shoemaker, so he could return in 1921 to San Marco and bring over his widowed mother. Lucky for me, he also brought back my own mother, whom he had fallen in love with on his brief trip home.

When they arrived in the States, my father had to pass through Ellis Island again—only this time he was a proud American citizen accompanying his young bride. It was a rough journey over for them. My mother came down with typhoid on the boat. When they got to Ellis she almost didn't pass inspection, but my father was a fast talker and convinced officials she was only seasick, so they let her through. My father took my mother to Allentown, where he lived the rest of his life. In fact, my mother's still there along with aunts and uncles and cousins.

Poets say the Statue of Liberty symbolized hope for the immigrant and Ellis Island, the reality. I know it did for my family—the reality of having to come to a foreign land, get educated, hang in there, and persevere under terrible odds. My parents took a risk when they came to this country and, in doing so, found a better life. For that, I will be forever grateful.

My family's beginning in this country is but one of thousands tied to Ellis Island. To me, the place holds as much history and more personal stories than any spot in America—twelve million, to be exact. That's the number of immigrants who landed at Ellis Island on their way to becoming Americans. These newcomers had a lot of children. Today we, their sons and daughters and grandchildren, number 100 million—almost half the nation.

Because so many people have deep roots in Ellis Island, our government decided to restore the place as a symbol of our nation's immigrant heritage. I am proud to have been a part of the project. It was a labor of love for me. A way of saying thanks to my parents for all they did. As founding chairman of The Statue of Liberty-Ellis Island Foundation, which raised the money to fix up the place, I found out that a lot of other folks felt the same way.

When people sent in donations, they always seemed to write me a letter. One man who was an immigrant said, "America has been good to me and I want to pay a little of it back." The second generation wrote, "Here's something for my mom and dad for all they went through for us."

Like me, people want to remember their family's story, and in restoring Ellis Island they have found a way to pass it on to their children and their children's children.

The words and photographs in this book also tell the story of what happened at Ellis Island when it welcomed millions to our shores. While the pictures are of Italians and Russians, Irish and Chinese, Jews and Greeks, the stories they tell are common ones of the bravery, determination, and spirit that characterized these newcomers.

◄ *Lee Iacocca, chairman of Chrysler Corporation, pauses at the balcony railing in the Great Hall on Ellis Island. As chairman of the Statue of Liberty-Ellis Island Foundation, he helped to raise approximately $230 million to restore and renovate the island's main building. (Photo by Tony Spina, courtesy of the* Detroit Free Press)

The men and women who landed at Ellis Island were as different as the nations from which they arrived. Infants and elderly, entire families, and single men and women. Most were young people no more than thirty years old. More men than women made the journey. Perhaps the only generalization you can make is that they were ordinary people who had made a not-so-ordinary decision, and in doing so formed the largest, most successful mass migration in modern history. And the reasons they came were just as varied.

Many sought steady work. Others wanted to be able to worship their God as they chose or escape political persecution. And then there were those who had come because they heard America's streets were paved with gold. While a lucky few struck it rich, most found that few, if any, streets were paved at all, and if they were, it was the immigrant who had done the work!

While America held out the promise of opportunity and freedom to these immigrants, the newcomers, in turn, offered much-needed labor to the country. In sweatshops and in coal fields, in factories and on the railroads, the immigrants labored, and as they did, they transformed the United States into the greatest industrial power in the world.

It is hard to imagine our country without the talents of these newcomers. We all benefit from their contributions. We listen to their music, read their books, and watch their plays and movies. Our food, architecture, language, and even our jokes have been shaped by those who came here in the last century.

Each time I visit Ellis Island, I am moved by the beauty of the place. As I walk the halls of the main building, I can almost hear the voices of those who passed through its doors. Now, of course, the rooms are filled with visitors and a magnificent museum that tells not only about the island, but also about all immigration to our country. To me, there is no more fitting place for this story to be told.

America's promise of opportunity would not have been realized without the courage, sacrifice, and hard work of the people who came through Ellis Island, but we also can't forget those who came long before. Their stories and those of contemporary immigrants are just as important. Since our country's beginnings, newcomers have always brought renewed energy to this land. Ellis Island is not just a monument to those who passed through its gates. It represents the hopes and aspirations of all people who came—and are still coming—to this country in search of the American Dream.

I hope that some day every American will have the opportunity to visit Ellis Island. But for those who can't, this book will provide an important chapter in our country's ongoing story of immigration.

Lee Iacocca

[xiii]

Prologue:
A Study in Contrasts

In 1990 a completely restored Ellis Island was rededicated by the National Park Service as a national monument and reopened for public use. For more than sixty years, from 1892 to 1954, the buildings on this small island in New York Harbor hosted the greatest migration in modern history. Indeed the story of Ellis Island is the story of American immigration. As the commissioner general of immigration observed in his annual report for 1927, "If the expressions 'Ellis Island' and 'immigration' were not synonymous, one could hardly think of the one without thinking of the other. Ellis Island was the great outpost of the new and vigorous Republic."

The story of Ellis Island and American immigration is best told in a book of black-and-white photos. Like history itself, the tones in the photographs range from inky black shadow to stark white light with myriad grays in between. The faces of the people pictured convey the gamut of emotional experience: joy and sorrow, happiness and despair, hope and fear. The photographs evince contrast in the buildings as well, from the high vaulted ceiling in the Great Hall to the crowded pens where the immigrants were detained. In this historical sequence of photographs we see the splendor of the newly constructed buildings degenerate into the squalor of an unused institution and then rise again to their former glory.

For the past century and a half the majority of immigrants to the United States have landed in New York Harbor. After October 28, 1886, they were greeted there by the magnificent monument that symbolized their journey—the Statue of Liberty. They were also greeted by immigration officials who shep-

herded the new hopefuls through the examination station. Beginning in 1892, the immigrants were brought to Ellis Island, which, like the Statue of Liberty, became a symbolic place for them. If the Statue of Liberty embodied their dreams of a new life with a bright future, then Ellis Island represented some of their darkest fears—of separation, rejection, and deportation.

American immigration is full of such contrasts. The Scottish writer Robert Louis Stevenson, who crossed the Atlantic with a shipload of immigrants, claimed that the men and women who left Europe were really all failures. Success having eluded them in the Old World, they were starting over in the New. Other commentators, remarking the opposite, portray the immigrants as the strongest and most courageous of the Old World stock—those willing to leave behind the familiar past for the challenge of an unknown future in an alien land.

Recollections of the voyage to America reflect a similar contradiction. Tales about the plight of immigrants in miserable steerage accommodations neglect to take into account the resilience of human nature. On every crossing sickness and suffering were tempered with hope. The whole life cycle was spanned on the voyage. There were births as well as deaths, though more often a preponderance of the latter. There were shipboard romances, marriages, and celebrations of birthdays and wedding anniversaries. The gaiety on board many of the ships was an expression of the joy with which the immigrants anticipated the future.

For the great majority the interlude on Ellis Island was a minor postponement of acceptance by the New World. Family reunions with husbands, wives, and other relatives long unseen took place there. But there were enough instances of poignant rejection to make Ellis Island a place of uncertainty and, therefore, trepidation. Stories about deportation and quar-

◀ *Approximately seventeen million immigrants passed through the Port of New York between 1892 and 1954; twelve million of them descended these stairs at Ellis Island to step successfully into America. (Photo by Wilton S. Tifft)*

Even the deplorable conditions often found in steerage accommodations could not dampen the spirits of new arrivals, as these voyagers in 1902 dancing on the deck of the SS Patricia *illustrate. (Photo courtesy of the Byron Collection, the Museum of the City of New York)*

antine had spread around Europe until some viewed Ellis as the "Island of Tears."

The positive side of the Ellis Island experience was clear from the outbursts of joy and hope by those who passed safely through. To the successful immigrants, passage through the examination meant certification of one's right to pursue a new life in the new land. For some that new life brought wealth beyond the wildest dreams of their friends and family left in the Old World. For others, however, a better life was not to be found; many immigrants lived and died in tenement-house squalor after arrival. Most fell into the great gray area between grandiosity and despair. But there was hope for all in the future generations of hyphenated Americans.

Contrast was also evident in the receptions accorded the immigrants when they came to America. American immigration played a vital role in the industrial, geographic, and urban growth that contributed to the development of the United States as a world power by the twentieth century. Nevertheless, resident Americans (some of whom themselves were not long off the boat) acted to limit the process of immigration severely, even as the fruits of that process led the nation to greatness. The United States has

long exhibited an ambivalent attitude toward her immigrants, one that "alternates between hospitality and paranoia . . . between a promiscuous inclusiveness and a nativist recoil." The restrictive side prevailed by the 1920s, and by the end of that decade Ellis Island became more a center of deportation than one of immigration.

The island closed in 1954 and quickly deteriorated into a place of rot and weeds. Vandals roamed its desolate halls while officials debated its disposition. Too important to discard, yet too expensive to restore, the island remained neglected until the United States' approaching Bicentennial refocused attention on America's past.

For nearly thirty years the island lay silent and empty, but Ellis Island was never really forgotten— not by those millions for whom it was the first contact with America and not by their children and grandchildren. Through the steady pressure of public opinion and the efforts of public officials and private citizens, Ellis Island again echoes with the sound of footsteps and the babble of voices. But they are the footsteps and the voices of the future for which the original twelve million risked so much.

In the registry room newcomers sat patiently waiting for their final examination. Passage meant certification of their individual rights to pursue new lives in their adopted homeland. (Photo courtesy of the National Park Service)

Passage through Ellis Island was an emotional experience. Feelings ranged from the trusting baby's enthusiastic salute in the middle of this photo to the cynical suspicion of the boy in the left foreground. Other immigrants were shy and somewhat fearful of the United States, as is the young girl hiding behind her hands in the right foreground. (Photo by Lewis W. Hine, courtesy of the New York Public Library)

ONE

The Island

The place known to millions of immigrants as Ellis Island has undergone myriad changes since the early seventeenth century, when New York Harbor became the site of exploration and settlement by Europeans. Claimed originally by the local Indians, the island subsequently passed under the control of Dutch settlers, English colonists, the state of New York, and the United States of America. It changed names half a dozen times in official documents and passed through the hands of countless private owners before the state of New York purchased the island and ceded it to the federal government in 1808. Even its size has changed dramatically. A mere three-acre blot of land in the harbor in 1600, the island has been steadily enlarged with landfill to its present size of 27½ acres. If history is defined as the process of change, Ellis Island certainly has a history.

When Henry Hudson sailed the *Half Moon* into New York Harbor in September 1609, he may have noticed the tiny island. If so, he did not think it sufficiently interesting to record. Hudson, exploring for the Dutch East India Company, was probably the third European to enter the area. It was perhaps symbolic of the later mixture of nationalities in New York that Hudson, an Englishman, sailed under the flag of the Netherlands, just as the Genoese Giovanni da Verrazano explored for France and Giovanni Caboto, whose name metamorphosed into the staid-sounding John Cabot, undertook voyages for England's Henry VII. (For that matter, Christopher Columbus was no Spaniard.)

Hudson assured himself a place in history and geography by sailing up the river later named for him in search of the Northwest Passage through the continent. Before embarking, however, he sent a

Visible from the barge dock and the main building, the Statue of Liberty not only beckoned immigrants to a new life of freedom and opportunity, but also served to encourage them throughout the tedious acceptance process on Ellis Island. (Photo by Wilton S. Tifft)

small boat ahead, with the crew in the charge of John Colman, to determine whether the river was deep enough for the safe passage of the *Half Moon*. When the boat was attacked by Indians, two crew members were seriously injured and Colman died with an arrow in his throat. From the beginning in New York Harbor, the going was tough for those Europeans who would seek their fortunes in America.

Hudson failed to find the Northwest Passage, but he did establish that the valley of the Hudson River was a fertile territory for settlement. In the 1620s the Dutch West India Company arrived with several families of Walloons, Protestants from the southern Netherlands (now Belgium). These people settled along the upper Hudson River, on Manhattan Island (dubbed New Amsterdam), and along the coasts of Long Island and Delaware.

Although Ellis Island was uninhabitable, lacking both fresh water and vegetation, the settlers, like the Indians before them, found other uses for it. Oyster fishermen used the island as a place to dry their nets. Picnickers found it pleasant for Sunday outings, where stylish Dutchmen drank ale and ate oysters plucked from the surrounding shoals. The Indians named the island Kioshk, or Gull Island, because of the birds attracted by the oysters around its shores. The Dutch, however, went directly to the source and dubbed it Little Oyster Island.

The Dutch period of colonization lasted only about thirty-five years. Indian attacks and authoritarian Dutch rule combined to discourage immigration to the colony. As Governor Peter Stuyvesant, beset by a multitude of problems, allowed colonial defenses to flag, the colony became ripe for plucking by the expansionist English. When their fleet sailed into the harbor in 1664, they took the colony without firing a shot. The new proprietor was James, Duke of York, for whom the colony was renamed.

Little Oyster Island belonged to a succession of private owners throughout the late 1600s, but then the

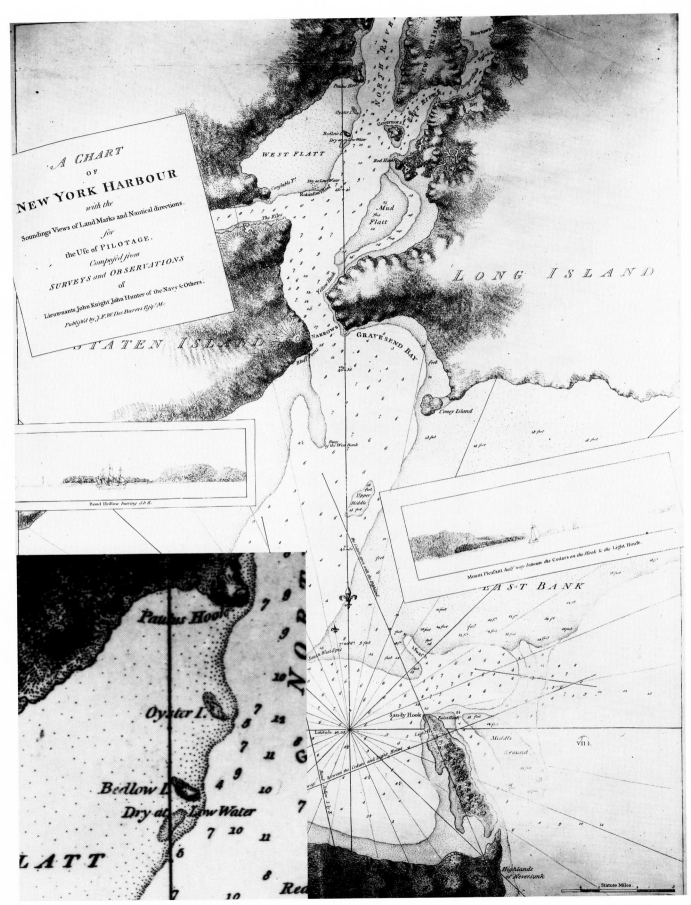

This sailing chart from 1781 outlines New York Harbor for seamen. The detail shows the location of Ellis Island, then one of the Oyster Islands, in the northeast corner of the western mud flat. (Chart courtesy of the Library of Congress)

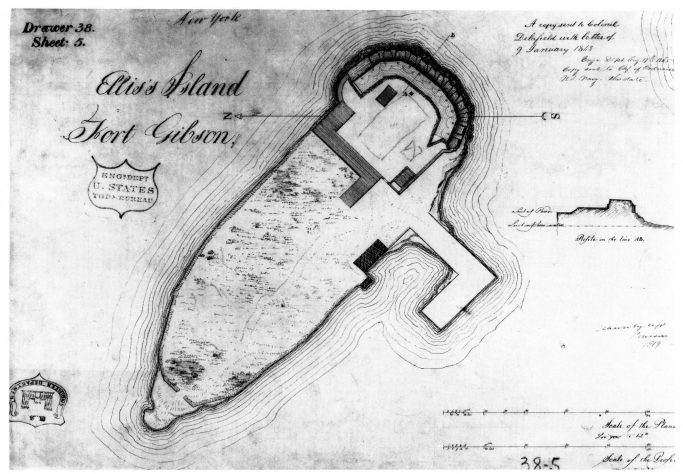

New York State purchased and then resold Ellis Island to the federal government in 1808. Shortly thereafter, the War Department (now the U.S. Defense Department) established a twenty-gun battery, a magazine, and a barracks on Ellis Island. However, it was not until 1834, when Congress ratified the compact of September 16, 1833, between New Jersey and New York, that state sovereignty over the island was finally established. Ellis and Bedloe's (now Liberty) islands would come under the jurisdiction of New York State even though they were closer to New Jersey. (Map courtesy of the Library of Congress)

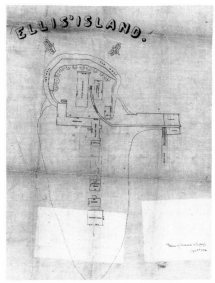

For years Ellis Island was known as Fort Gibson. This map shows the layout of the fort. Fort Gibson was dismantled prior to the Civil War and a naval powder magazine was established on the site. (Map courtesy of the Library of Congress)

record of private ownership vanishes, not to reappear until almost a century later. In between, the island, called Dyre's or Bucking Island in some eighteenth-century documents, became a base for the commercial exploitation of shad and herring. Because of this, the island occasionally served as a site for the punishment of pirates. It then became known as Gibbet or Anderson's Island. Sometimes pirates were hanged on Manhattan, and their bodies suspended from the gibbet on Gibbet Island as a warning to sailors about the negative prospects of a career in piracy.

The first eighteenth-century record of the island's private ownership is dated 1785, when Samuel Ellis put the island up for sale. A New Jersey farm owner who also engaged in assorted mercantile activities in Manhattan, Ellis operated a tavern for fishermen on Ellis Island. In 1785 he advertised the island and a variety of merchandise for sale. He failed to sell the island before his death in 1794 and willed it to his descendants.

That same year the island became a component

THE EXPANSION OF ELLIS ISLAND

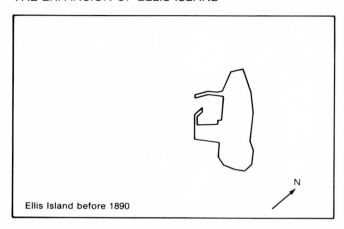

Ellis Island before 1890

Ellis Island underwent drastic physical changes over the years. Originally it was a three-acre plot of land that was purchased from the Indians by the Dutch in 1630. Known for the oyster beds surrounding it and despite its near-disappearance at high tide, the island served as the base for a growing commercial fishing industry until it was sold to the U.S. government in 1808.

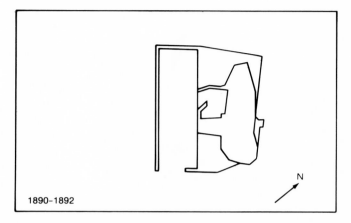

1890–1892

On April 11, 1890, Congress appropriated $75,000 to remove a naval magazine and permit the Treasury Department to improve Ellis Island so that a federal immigration station could be built there. Added landfill more than doubled the original 3.3-acre site.

in the defense of the harbor and the city when New York City ceded their island to the state of New York. The French Revolution had brought about a nationalistic rivalry in Europe that led to a protracted period of warfare. Since the United States traded on a large scale with the belligerent nations, government officials feared maritime incidents might draw the reluctant republic into the hostilities. Thus fortifications were necessary in the large Atlantic coastal harbors, including New York. In April 1795 the New York state legislature appropriated $100,000 to fortify Governor's Island, Bedloe's Island, and Ellis Island. However, construction on Ellis Island was hampered by the question of ownership.

In 1807, tensions with England reached the boiling point, and, after surveying the defenses of New York Harbor, the chief engineer of the U.S. Army recommended that additional fortifications be built on Ellis Island. New York governor Daniel Tompkins set out to acquire the island by passing legislation that would subject it to condemnation. This accomplished, the state appointed a commission "of the most respectable kind and generally esteemed good judges of property" to determine a fair price for the island. The distinguished jury set a price of $10,000 to satisfy all the claimants and clear the title. On June 30, 1808, the governor executed a deed transferring the title and all rights in Ellis Island to the federal government for a sum of $10,183.10. The deed was then delivered to the Secretary of War.

After acquiring unrestricted title to Ellis Island, the government built a small fortress containing a twenty-gun battery, a magazine, and a barracks for troops. Although the fortification known as Fort Gib-

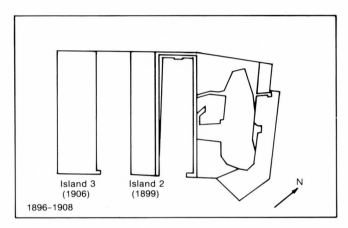

Island 3
(1906)
Island 2
(1899)

1896-1908

N

In 1897 the original Ellis Island buildings, through which 1.5 million immigrants had passed, were destroyed by fire. The architectural firm of Boring & Tilton designed the fireproof structures seen today. The buildings are in the French Renaissance style, featuring laid-in Flemish bond with limestone trim. More landfill created Islands Number 2 and Number 3, which were joined by a common causeway. The hospital complex and the contagious diseases buildings were added during this period of construction.

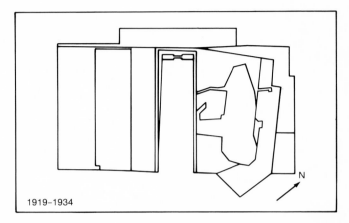

1919-1934

N

The inlet bay between Islands Number 2 and Number 3 was filled in to provide recreational areas for patients, and new concrete-and-granite seawalls were installed. Playgrounds and landscaping throughout the three-island complex also were added. Ellis Island's last major construction period benefited from both the coffers and the laborers of the Public Works Administration. Landfill produced recreation grounds on the Manhattan side of Ellis Island's main building. (Illustrations by Rosemary Morrissey-Herzberg)

son did not see action during the War of 1812, the Ellis Island barracks did house British prisoners as well as American soldiers.

After the war Fort Gibson lay quiet. It was home to a few recruits, and a few more pirates met their ends there. The fort served little military purpose during peacetime but was maintained in case it might be needed in some future defense of the harbor. In 1861 Fort Gibson was dismantled and a naval magazine was set up in its place. When the Civil War broke out, the island was put to use as a supply depot for dispatching powder and shells to naval vessels.

Following the Civil War the island was immersed in controversy. Charles Dana's ever-vigilant and waspish *New York Sun* shocked its readers with the warning that New Yorkers and their property were in imminent danger of annihilation should an

explosion occur in the Ellis Island powder stores. *Harper's Weekly* titillated its readers with figures: three thousand barrels and assorted shells were stored on the island. The magazine carried a sketch of the masonry-walled buildings where the powder was stored, along with details about the destructive power of such a large quantity of explosive material. A New Jersey congressman, fearing that an inopportune bolt of lightning could ignite the powder and destroy lower Manhattan, Staten Island, and eastern New Jersey, introduced a resolution in Congress calling for the navy's abandonment of Ellis Island.

The resolution failed, and the arsenal remained on Ellis Island. Despite the controversy the island itself saw very little activity after the Civil War and remained a quiet, nearly deserted place, waiting for history to happen to it again.

Two

American Immigration:
People and Policies to 1890

It may be a cliché to remark that the United States is a nation of immigrants, but it must be remembered that a cliché is simply an often-stated truth. From the first English settlements at Jamestown in 1607 and Plymouth in 1620 arose a nation of some 2.5 million white settlers by the time of the American Revolution. All were immigrants or direct descendants of immigrants. All were not, however, English.

Growth and expansion meant increased production and wealth in the American colonies, so immigrants were generally welcome. Thousands of English Puritans descended on the Massachusetts Bay colony in its first decade, such a great influx that the main source of income in the colony was selling supplies to the newcomers.

This does not mean, however, that all immigrants were welcome in all colonies. A group of Walloons who petitioned to join the Jamestown colony in 1621 were accepted only with the injunction that they limit their number to three hundred and conform to the Church of England. French Huguenots and German Palatines faced similar restrictions in most colonies in the seventeenth century. Welsh Quakers faced death if they wandered from the friendly confines of Pennsylvania into the dour Puritan towns of Massachusetts Bay.

Some colonies were less provincial than others. New York was one of the most cosmopolitan. The Dutch had absorbed the New Sweden colony and its smattering of Swedes and Finns prior to English conquest. Frenchmen from Canada and the Caribbean, Spanish traders, Portuguese Jews, Scotch voyagers,

◀ *A burgeoning population coupled with changing social and economic conditions in Europe prompted many, like this Irish immigrant on the quay of Dublin in 1854, to pursue the promise of land and work in America. (Lithograph by T. H. Maguire after a painting by T. Nichol, courtesy of the New York Historical Society)*

and a variety of Germans added to the ethnic stew. When the Duke of York assumed proprietorship, eighteen languages were spoken in his colony.

The eighteenth century brought new settlers to America, including thousands of Scotch-Irish and Germans who settled in farming communities throughout the colonies. However most of the immigrants during this period came as unfree labor. It has been estimated that 75 percent of the white immigrants between 1700 and 1780 were indentured servants who would spend years working off the price of their passage. The slave trade also flourished. Nearly 300,000 blacks were brought from Africa between 1714 and 1808, when Congress outlawed the importation of slaves.

The early years of the new republic saw a greater acceptance of diversity, reflected in the famous words of Michel-Guillaume-Jean de Crèvecoeur, the first writer to advance the image of America as a melting pot. "What then is the American, this new man?" he asked in 1782. "Here individuals of all nations are melted into a new race of men, whose labours and posterity will one day cause great changes in the world."

For nearly half a century from the time de Crèvecoeur extolled the ethnic diversity of the United States, the admixture of national stocks remained more or less constant. According to the 1790 census, people of English descent comprised 60 percent of the population, Germans and Scotch about 8 percent each, Irish and Scotch-Irish 17 percent, with smaller numbers of Dutch, French, and Scandinavians. While the white population increased from around three million in the 1770s to nearly thirteen million by 1830, the gain was due mostly to the hardiness and fecundity of the native population rather than to large-scale immigration. This would change dramatically during the rest of the nineteenth century as millions fled worsening economic, social, and polit-

From the 1830s until the eve of the Civil War, 39 percent of those immigrating to the United States were fleeing the blighted potato fields of Ireland. Faced with hardship and possible starvation at home, these Irish emigrants on the quay of Cork on May 10, 1851, are part of the 1.9 million Irish who risked the perilous voyage for a better life in America. (Illustration from the Illustrated London Times, *courtesy of the New York Public Library)*

This 1840 drawing illustrates the congestion on an old sailing vessel crossing the Atlantic. The federal government's first attempt at regulating immigration (1848) addressed the deplorable conditions found aboard passenger ships. Unfortunately the law did not regulate passengers carried in steerage. (Illustration courtesy of Brown Brothers)

This is an early illustration of New York Harbor. The East River, Castle Garden, which served as the harbor's immigration station from 1855 to 1890, and the Battery are visible in the background (center) of the drawing. (Illustration courtesy of the New York Public Library)

The call went out throughout northern Europe that America needed people to settle its expanding frontier. The response brought many more Catholics into American society and caused concern among native-born Americans. Many of these French emigrants on the dock of the Compagnie Générale Transatlantique at Le Havre in 1886 were probably Catholics. (Illustration by E. Clair-Guyat, courtesy of the New York Public Library)

Having survived the crossing, the immigrants' spirit remained undaunted as their belongings were unloaded at the Castle Garden dock. Notice the wooden trunk depicted in the lower right corner of this painting. It reads "Pat Murfy for Ameriky." (Painting by Samuel Wauch, courtesy of the Museum of the City of New York)

ical conditions in Europe to seek land, opportunity, and freedom in the New World.

The massive migration consisted of three separate waves, the first of which began in the 1830s and continued until the eve of the Civil War. The second wave started shortly after the Civil War and continued into the 1890s. The third, and largest, wave began in 1900 and lasted until World War I.

The first wave was triggered by territorial acquisitions. The 1803 Louisiana Purchase doubled the size of the United States, and by 1853 its present continental boundaries had been established through a series of annexations. Landowning railroads, territorial governments, and land speculators, anxious to encourage settlement of the West, sent agents to Europe to actively promote immigration. By 1860, more than five million newcomers had arrived in America, many of them bound for the new territory. Fully 90 percent of these first-wave immigrants came from northern and western Europe, with the bulk from Ireland (39 percent) and Germany (31 percent). Scandinavians, particularly Norwegians, also came in large numbers during this period.

"On the boat we came in steerage. Third class was plain steerage. . . . They piled us up eight or ten people in one cabin, and the food was the worst that it could be."
—Sam Auspitz, emigrated from Czechoslovakia in 1920

The millions who stepped off the ships into a new life were the lucky ones. Many who began the journey to America never finished it. From the beginning, the ocean voyage to America was long, arduous, and perilous. A fatality rate of 10 to 15 percent was not uncommon. A few mid-eighteenth-century horror stories told of crossings during which half the passengers perished. Gottlieb Mittelberger, a German who made the voyage to Philadelphia in 1750, described a trip that lasted six months "amid such hardships as no one is able to describe adequately with their misery":

. . . stench, fumes, horror, vomiting, many kinds of seasickness, fever, dysentery, headache, heat, constipation, boils, scurvy, cancer, mouth-rot, and the like, all of which came from old and sharply salted food and meat, also from very bad and foul water, so that many die miserably.

Add to this want of provisions, hunger, thirst, frost, heat, dampness, anxiety, want, afflictions and lamentations, together with other trouble, the lice abound so frightfully, especially on sick people, that they can be scraped off the body. The misery reaches the climax when a gale rages for two or three nights and days, so that everyone believes that the ship will go to the bottom with all human beings on board. In such a visitation the people cry and pray most piteously.

The hideous conditions of the voyage did not improve substantially during the following century. In 1819, as a result of such reports, the federal government set limits on the number of passengers a ship could carry and levied fines against the shipping line of $150 for every passenger over the limit. The law also specified minimum amounts of water and provisions to be carried and set fines for shortages. Customs collectors in American ports were designated to keep statistics on numbers of passengers and their ports of origin, a practice that inaugurated federal recordkeeping of numbers of incoming immigrants.

The glaring deficiency in this law was that it did not regulate passengers carried in steerage—the below-decks section of the ship named for its proximity to the steering apparatus—or on the orlop deck. The orlop deck was located in the very bottom of the vessel; planks placed across the ship served as both the floor of steerage and the ceiling of the orlop deck. The passengers who were crammed tightly into these areas, where the head clearance was only five feet, suffered from a lack of sanitary facilities and from poor ventilation. The only air received below decks came through the hatches, which were fastened down during stormy weather. Prior to 1848, when Congress required shipping lines to provide cooked food to passengers, immigrants were instructed to carry their own food for the voyage. Woe to those who did not bring enough!

By the mid-1800s many citizens were critical of the treatment accorded new arrivals in New York Harbor. Consequently, New York established the Board of Commissioners of Emigration to oversee immigration at the port. A top priority was to protect immigrants from the unscrupulous. A fort and theater, Castle Garden became one of the country's earliest immigration stations in 1855. This overview of New York and Brooklyn shows Castle Garden before Battery Park was filled in. (Illustration courtesy of the New York Public Library)

Not only would immigrants have to load their personal belongings, but prior to 1848, when Congress required shipping lines to provide cooked food to passengers, immigrants were instructed to bring along their own food for the voyage. A typical list for a family of five included 672 pounds of potatoes, 280 pounds of flour, 20 pounds of butter, 20 pounds of bacon, 50 pounds of dried fish, and 14 pounds of sugar. (Illustration courtesy of Brown Brothers)

Deadly typhus (called "ship fever" when contracted at sea) was the common result when poor food was combined with lack of fresh air and sanitation. One nineteenth-century writer observed that the dead were "thrown into the ocean with as little ceremony as old sacks or broken tools." He commented further that "If crosses and tombstones could be erected on the water . . . the whole route of the emigrant vessel from Europe to America would long since have assumed the appearance of crowded cemeteries."

In view of such conditions, it is small wonder that early federal regulations attempted to ameliorate problems faced by immigrants. Some state governments also took measures to safeguard the immigrants. The leader in this respect was the state of New York.

By the middle of the 1840s many citizens were critical of the treatment accorded new arrivals in New York Harbor. Such criticism led the state legislature to appoint a special committee of investigation, which reported in 1847 on the numerous frauds perpetrated against immigrants. The commission found that boardinghouse keepers hired "runners" to steer immigrants to their establishments. Paid according to the number of newcomers they could attract, the runners often seized the immigrants' luggage, or even small children, forcing their victims to give chase. Once they arrived at the boardinghouses, the immigrants were grossly overcharged, and many were robbed of their valuables. Confidence men of other sorts also preyed on the newcomers, selling them spurious train and boat tickets. When these findings

In the Rotunda, or Great Hall, of Castle Garden immigrants were interviewed before acceptance. The room had fifty thousand square feet of floor space under a seventy-five-foot-high domed ceiling. The procedures developed here would eventually be adopted at all immigrant examining stations. (Woodcut from Harper's Monthly, *April 1871 issue, courtesy of the New York Public Library)*

After registering, immigrants could purchase railroad and boat tickets from approved agents in the building. However, many of them stayed in New York, more than doubling the city's population to 814,000 in 1860. (Engraving courtesy of the Museum of the City of New York)

Unschooled newcomers could solicit assistance from the Letter-Writing Department, which helped them send news of their arrival to relatives and friends. To help immigrants find employment the board of commissioners established the Labor Exchange, operated free of charge. (Engraving from sketches by Stanley Fox in Harper's Weekly, courtesy of the Library of Congress)

were digested, along with those of another commission investigating conditions in poorhouses and hospitals for indigent immigrants, a beleaguered state legislature established the Board of Commissioners of Emigration, which was charged with overseeing immigration in New York.

The board of commissioners set out to inspect, count, and protect immigrants entering the state. One of its first achievements was acquiring part of Ward's Island in the East River (opposite 100th to 116th streets) for hospital accommodations for sick immigrants. This removed the infirm from the greedy hands of private interests, which had formerly taken state monies and provided the shabbiest treatment imaginable.

In 1848 the commissioners leased a pier at the end of Hubert Street. This second measure was aimed at protecting immigrants from runners and confidence men while the newcomers landed and made their travel connections. However, local residents complained about the resulting loss of their quiet neighborhood and, in 1855, board members moved to secure Castle Garden, located on a narrow strip of landfill on the southwestern tip of the Battery. Originally built as a fort, Castle Garden had, more recently, served as an opera house that hosted Jenny Lind.

Castle Garden was one of the country's earliest immigrant receiving stations. The first immigrants landed there two days after it opened in 1855. By the end of the year the commissioners reported that 51,114 persons had "been landed safely, without accident to themselves or property." The procedure for immigrants at Castle Garden was similar to later processes at Ellis Island. Ships entering the harbor were first met at the Quarantine Station six miles below the city, where officers reported on the number of passengers and deaths, health conditions, and the cleanliness of the ships. The ships then proceeded to piers, where members of the Landing Department supervised the transfer of passengers and baggage to smaller boats, which landed at the Castle Garden pier. The sick were transferred to hospitals.

At Castle Garden the immigrants entered the Rotunda, the huge circular central hall, seventy-five feet high. There they were interviewed by officials who gathered basic information: name, nationality, former residence, and destination in the United States. After registering, immigrants could purchase railroad and boat tickets from approved agents in the building, without fear of fraud. Board-approved money changers operated at Castle Garden as well, exchanging all types of foreign currency for U.S. dollars and cents at current market rates. Baggage was sorted for shipment to boats and trains for minimal fees.

Various other services were also provided at Castle Garden. Immigrants unfamiliar with the geogra-

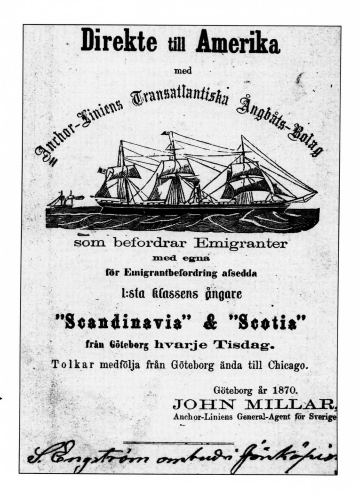

Scandinavian advertisements offered emigrants ▶ *employment agencies, money changers, and language teachers aboard ship. The Great Lakes region, with its $1.50-an-acre land, $40 horses, and $10 cows, appealed to them. (Poster courtesy of the Minnesota Historical Society)*

Pre–Civil War immigration peaked between 1846 and 1855, when the nation welcomed more than three million new residents. Although immigration declined during the Civil War, immigrants who did come were often met at the Battery by Union army recruiting officers offering them inducements to enlist. (Engraving courtesy of the New York Public Library)

phy of their adopted country could find assistance in the Information Department. (This agency could not solve all the problems of understanding, however. Many immigrants arrived with only the name of a town where their relatives were located, and these names were frequently duplicated in four or five states or territories.) Those unschooled individuals who wished to send news of their arrival to relatives back home could solicit aid from the Letter-Writing Department. The board of commissioners even established a Labor Exchange, operated free of charge, to assist immigrants in finding employment. By 1870, when approximately 70 percent of European immigrants entered the United States through New York, Castle Garden was open day and night. The facility employed seventy-six people, with an annual salary total of $82,894.

The task of receiving immigrants at Castle Garden in the early years of its use was made easier by falling numbers of ships and passengers. Pre–Civil War immigration peaked between 1846 and 1855, when the country received over three million new arrivals. In the following decade, from 1856 to 1865,

the total dropped to 1.65 million. Clearly the problems that presaged the war, as well as the war itself, made America less attractive to prospective immigrants. But immediately after the war the floodgates reopened and immigrants poured through in unprecedented numbers:

1866 to 1870	1.5 million
1871 to 1875	1.7 million
1876 to 1880	1.1 million
1881 to 1885	3.0 million
1886 to 1890	2.3 million

This second great wave of the nineteenth century again consisted mainly of British (20 percent), Germans (30 percent), Irish (15 percent), and Scandinavians (10 percent). This new group of immigrants required little incentive to come to America other than the country's burgeoning economy. During the last third of the century the United States became one of the great producing nations of the world, and industrial expansion required a vast labor force. As historian Marcus Lee Hansen has pointed out, one of the few generalizations that apply to American immigration is that "periods of greatest volume corresponded with the eras of liveliest industrial activity in the United States."

Coupled with the availability of employment was the fact that the voyage to the United States was becoming less of a death-defying act for steerage passengers. Conditions on the ships were not greatly improved, but travel time was shorter. By 1870 nearly half the voyages across the Atlantic were made in steam-powered vessels, which made the passage in ten to fourteen days in contrast to the weeks-long voyages of the older sailing ships. (After the turn of the century, this time was reduced further to seven to ten days.) Less time in steerage meant reduced risk of contracting contagious diseases like cholera and smallpox. Less time in a filthy hole with little air and minimal food supplies reduced the danger of succumbing to typhus.

Perhaps the best description of a late-nineteenth-century crossing is that of Robert Louis Stevenson, the Scottish writer. While he booked a second-class cabin in order to have a writing table while crossing, he seemed to have spent most of his time with the

Following the Civil War, immigrants flocked to New York Harbor once more. In 1866, when this engraving was done, the wave that would bring 1.5 million to Castle Garden by 1870 had already begun. (Engraving courtesy of the Museum of the City of New York)

steerage passengers, for whom he displayed a genuine interest and fondness. He observed that the price differential between second class and steerage was minuscule. The real thing separating the two groups of passengers was their treatment aboard the ship. As he wryly observed, "In the steerage there are males and females; in the second class ladies and gentlemen."

The ship's violent motion and lack of fresh air in the steerage section promoted an epidemic of seasickness, according to Stevenson. He estimated that two or three of every five steerage passengers suffered from it. He described the descent into Steerage Section Number 1 as "an adventure that required some nerve. The stench was atrocious; each respiration tasted in the throat like some horrible kind of cheese." In spite of such conditions, most of the passengers there were cheerful and optimistic about the future. They entertained themselves daily with music and dancing.

Not all of the shortcomings of the steerage passage were physical. There was a psychological dimension as well, which Stevenson observed on an otherwise carefree afternoon of singing and dancing:

Through this merry and good-hearted scene there came three cabin passengers, a gentleman and two young ladies, picking their way with little gracious titters of indulgence, and a Lady-Bountiful air about nothing, which galled me to the quick. I have little of the radical in social

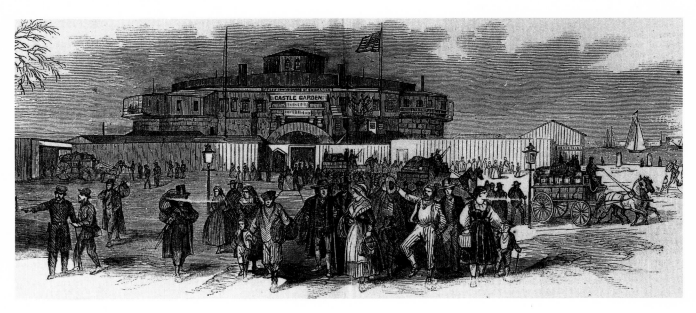

Between 1866 and 1890 more than nine million people emigrated to America's shores, where labor was scarce and wages were relatively high as compared to those in Europe. Women, especially, were courted to fill jobs in the United States' expanding textile mills. Here, a father or brother tries to prevent the young woman from leaving for America. (Engraving courtesy of the New York Public Library)

questions, and have always nourished an idea that one person was as good as another. But I began to be troubled by this episode. It was astonishing what insults these people managed to convey by their presence. They seemed to throw their clothes in our faces. Their eyes searched us all over for tatters and incongruities. A laugh was ready at their lips; but they were too well-mannered to indulge it in our hearing. Wait a bit, till they were all back in the salon, and then hear how wittily they would depict the manners of the steerage. We were in truth very innocently, cheerfully, and sensibly engaged, and there was no shadow of excuse for the swaying elegant superiority with which these damsels passed among us, or for the stiff and waggish glances of their squire. Not a word was said; only when they were gone Mackay sullenly damned their impudence under his breath; but we were all conscious of an icy influence and a dead break in the course of our enjoyment.

In the years immediately after the Civil War nativists, those opposed to an open immigration pol-

icy, were neither as pervasive nor as persuasive as they had been during the previous wave of immigration. Immigrants were easily absorbed into northern factory towns and cities, the West offered plentiful space for immigrant farmers, and the South tried, albeit unsuccessfully, to lure newcomers into the cotton and tobacco fields formerly worked by slaves. Immigrants were seen by Americans not as a detriment to the country but as a valuable resource. In 1870 one New York commissioner of immigration estimated that newcomers increased the wealth of the United States by some $400 million annually.

The increasing economic importance of immigration again brought the federal government into the picture. "An Act to Regulate Immigration" passed Congress and received presidential approval in 1882. It recognized the secretary of the Treasury as the official responsible for the regulation of immigration and empowered him to enter into agreements with state officials to implement the law. Immigrants excluded by the act were "any convict, lunatic, idiot, or any person unable to take care of himself or herself without becoming a public charge." (This was actually the third exclusion law. The first two mainly

By 1870 nearly half of the voyages across the Atlantic were made in steamships. The coal- and wood-stoked steam-powered vessels could traverse the Atlantic Ocean in ten to fourteen days, while sailing ships often took weeks. This Currier and Ives engraving looking out from the Battery illustrates both the old and the newer ships in Upper and Lower New York Bay. (Engraving courtesy of the Museum of the City of New York)

placed restrictions on the large numbers of Chinese immigrants entering through the Pacific ports. The exclusion of this ethnic group continued in some form until 1952.)

Once the federal legislative process was rolling, it proved difficult to stop. The next act passed was the Alien Contract Labor Law (1885), which prohibited the practice of importing aliens under terms of a contract for employment made prior to their importation. The act was promoted by reformers who wished to prevent the exploitation of immigrants and by the labor movement, which wanted to halt the importation of cheap foreign labor. The law represented one of the finest nineteenth-century examples of the paradox of conflicting interests in a liberal democracy—a country that feared an influx of indigents turned away immigrants who had guaranteed jobs.

Federal regulations affected the Port of New York more than any other because of the high percentage of immigrants who entered there. Castle Garden, a fine facility in its time, was not large enough to handle the inflated numbers of the 1880s. A congressional committee visited the facility in 1888 and found it quite unsatisfactory:

The committee visited Castle Garden on several occasions and witnessed the arrival and inspection of immigrants, and it was very obvious to them that it was almost impossible to properly inspect the large number of persons who arrive daily during the immigrant season. . . . Large numbers of persons not lawfully entitled to land in the United States are annually received at this port. In fact, one of the commissioners of immigration himself testified that the local administration of affairs at Castle Garden, by the method and system now followed, was a perfect farce.

This 1889 report concluded by supporting a view that many had been urging for years: "The regulation of immigration is a matter affecting the whole Union, and is pre-eminently a proper subject for Federal control." Consequently the secretary of the Treasury terminated the government's contract with the board of commissioners in 1890 and assumed sole authority in immigration matters in New York. The search for a better procedure would culminate in the construction of a new immigration facility on Ellis Island.

From 1855 until 1890 immigrants entered America via Castle Garden, but it was shot through with corruption. Staffers and outsiders often took advantage of immigrants' language difficulties, culture shock, and travel-induced exhaustion to steal their money and possessions. (Photo courtesy of the New York Public Library)

Public outrage over the scandalous exploitation and ▶ seriously inadequate facilities at Castle Garden caused the federal government to cancel its contract with the New York Board of Commissioners of Emigration. Castle Garden closed as an immigration station in 1890. By 1906, when this photograph was taken, the former immigration station had reopened as an aquarium. (Photo by the H. C. White Co., courtesy of the Library of Congress)

◀ As illustrated here, early-model steamships had both stacks and the sails of the older clipper ships. This White Star Line advertisement was printed by an Irish agency in the 1880s. (Poster courtesy of the National Park Service, Statue of Liberty National Monument)

THREE

Building and Rebuilding
an Immigration Station

In the 1890s American immigration reached a turning point. As the federal government assumed control of the process, new policies and procedures were effected, leading to a more thorough examination of passengers. The flow of immigration also changed, as a higher percentage of newcomers came from places other than northern and western Europe. One part of the process remained the same: New York Harbor continued to be the primary port of entry—almost 80 percent of all immigrants disembarked there in the 1890s. Ellis Island, which officially opened on the first day of 1892, would serve as the premier immigration facility in the United States through the most intensive period of foreign arrivals in American history.

The selection of the new site had not been easy. Treasury Secretary William Windom favored the use of one of the many government-owned islands in the harbor. Such a site would insulate the immigrants from the assorted sharpsters and thieves who would take advantage of their ignorance of the language and local customs. After visiting New York, he settled on Bedloe's Island—a choice that immediately became a matter of public interest and heated controversy. Bedloe's Island already served as the site for the Statue of Liberty. A gift from the people of France, the monumental statue had been unveiled with impressive ceremony on October 28, 1886. Truly a people's tribute to liberty, the statue had been erected at a cost of $270,000, $100,000 contributed by the "wealthy" and

During the last half of the nineteenth century the forces for change in Europe had been moving inexorably south and east. By the time the federal government began building its new immigration station on Ellis Island in 1890, the faces and languages of the newly arrived immigrants began to change. More and more southern and eastern Europeans, like this Romanian woman, were stepping off the boats seeking a better life in America. (Photo courtesy of the National Park Service)

the balance by 120,000 Americans (mostly schoolchildren) in response to a fund-raising campaign in Joseph Pulitzer's *New York World.* Now, inspired by strident editorials in the *World,* a wave of protesters argued that a station monitoring the arrival of the poor and oppressed of the world would deface the island where the Statue of Liberty extended her welcome. A New York City alderman introduced a resolution decrying the plan as a "wanton act of violence." A majority of his fellow aldermen agreed and passed the resolution. Meanwhile, Governor's Island was rejected because of opposition from the army.

Ellis Island won mainly by default. Secretary Windom had originally rejected it when he visited New York because the water surrounding it was so shallow that his boat could not get within a hundred yards of it. This did not bode well for landing shiploads of immigrants. In addition, the island was too low for any substantial building projects. The island was, however, available, and there was no opposition to its use. In fact, the controversial munitions dump on Ellis Island was again under attack. Opponents of the munitions dump would favor use of the island for any alternative purpose. Consequently, on April 11, 1890, President Benjamin Harrison signed a bill calling for the removal of the munitions and the preparation of Ellis Island as an immigration station.

The transformation of Ellis Island began with optimistic predictions that it would be open for business early in 1891. (In fact, the opening did not take place until early 1892.) The federal superintendent of public buildings visited the island in mid-April 1890 and pronounced five of the existing buildings usable, "with slight alterations." He also noted, however, that the shallowness of the water would necessitate a landing pier several hundred feet long. In addition, an artesian well several hundred feet deep was needed to provide fresh water for the island. In spite of plans to proceed immediately in April, contracts were not

signed until August, and it was November 10, 1890, when the New York firm of Sheridan & Byrne won the contracting rights to build the main building and boiler house (at a cost of $280,000).

Meanwhile immigrants continued to arrive daily. With Castle Garden unavailable, Treasury authorities transferred their operations temporarily to the Barge Office in lower Manhattan's Battery Park. Less than a decade old, the Barge Office had been built for the convenience of cabin-class passengers, who were ferried there by barges (thus the name) to pass through customs. However, as the steamship companies preferred to land passengers directly at docks in New York and New Jersey, it was little used. After a quick remodeling job the Barge Office received its first passengers on April 19, only a few weeks after the decision to relocate from Castle Garden.

The first immigrants to enter the refurbished building were 734 steerage passengers from the Hamburg-America steamer *Columbia*. First through was Herman Volke, a thirty-six-year-old locksmith from Saxe-Weimar-Eisenach. After receiving a $5 gold piece from the commissioner of immigration, he proclaimed his intention of traveling to Pittsburgh with his wife, dog, and cat.

While the federal government had already assumed responsibility for immigration in New York, the Immigration Act of 1891 extended this condition to the rest of the nation, affecting existing policies everywhere. The new law, enacted in March, excluded more classes of immigrants. Denied entry were "idiots, insane persons, paupers or persons likely to become a public charge, persons suffering from a loathsome or a dangerous contagious disease, persons who have been convicted of a felony or other infamous crime or misdemeanor involving moral turpitude, polygamists," and those whose passage was paid by someone other than a relative or friend. Persons convicted of "a political offense" were specifically not excluded under the act. Advertising to solicit emigrants by steamship companies and by prospective employers was barred. Deportation policy was better defined, and the cost of transporting deportees back to their ports of origin was made the responsibility of the shipping companies that brought them, clearly an

unpopular provision with these companies. Most important was the provision placing authority over all U.S. immigration in the hands of the superintendent of immigration, supervised by the secretary of the Treasury. The first superintendent, appointed in April 1891, was a former Republican congressman from Indiana, William D. Owen.

The new law had less effect in New York than elsewhere, as the Treasury Department had been in charge of operations in New York for more than a year. The commissioner of immigration in New York was Colonel John B. Weber, a businessman from Buffalo, who remained in office after the passage of the new law. Most accounts indicate that Weber was

Steamship companies, such as Compagnie Générale Transatlantique, tried to lure passengers to the New World with idealized advertisements such as this one. The Immigration Act of 1891 barred the companies from actively recruiting immigrant passengers. (Poster courtesy of the New York Public Library)

Immigrants and cartmen wait outside the Barge Office around 1900. From 1890 to 1892, when the Ellis Island facility was opened, immigrants were processed at the Barge Office. After the fire in 1897, it was back to the Barge Office for three years while fireproof buildings were completed on Ellis Island. (Photo courtesy of the Byron Collection, Museum of the City of New York)

an honest and judicious official who succeeded largely by applying business practices to the process of examining immigrants. At least one contemporary account, however, viewed his appointment with a jaundiced eye, claiming he was the tool of New York boss Tom Platt and was not particularly qualified for the job. The *New York Times* observed, "He has been a beggar for public office ever since he was old enough to fill one" and concluded that Weber "has always been in politics for what he could get out of it."

In fact, Commissioner Weber performed creditably in office. He maintained good relations with the Treasury Department (something his successors did not always achieve) and operated efficiently, given the limitations of the Barge Office. In June 1891 he was dispatched to Europe to head the Foreign Immigration Commission, which studied conditions at the source to better understand the nature of American immigration. Weber's reports were important in shaping subsequent immigration policy.

Construction on Ellis Island proceeded through-

out 1891. The island was more than doubled in size by driving piles in the shallow waters around it and filling the gaps with earth from nearby areas and ballast from ships coming into the harbor. The old naval ammunition depot was removed and the ground leveled. Workers converted five buildings and erected seven, including the main building, a hospital, a powerhouse, surgeon's quarters, a bathhouse, and a detention building.

The centerpiece of construction was, of course, the main building. Clearly visible from Battery Park, it was described by *Harper's Weekly* as looking like "a latter-day watering place hotel, presenting to the view a great many-windowed expanse of buff-painted wooden walls, of blue slate roofing, and of light and picturesque towers." The huge three-story building, "of no particular style of architecture," according to the *New York Times*, had a floor space on both the ground and second floors that measured more than 400 by 150 feet. The first floor consisted of baggage-handling rooms and railway ticket offices and waiting rooms. The second floor contained registry clerks

When weather permitted, passengers would escape the cramped steerage quarters and lounge on deck. Each hoped to be the first to sight the Statue of Liberty. Bedloe's Island, which served as the site for Miss Liberty, was also proposed as a possible site for the new federal immigration station. That idea was quickly squashed. (Photo courtesy of the National Archives)

seated at desks at the head of each of ten aisles, where immigrants lined up to answer the questions required by immigration laws. The third floor, called the balcony floor, was open to the second floor and allowed for inspection without contact.

Rising from each corner of the main building and adding to the majestic look of the place was a square, four-story tower with a pyramidal roof. The towers contained administrative offices, including those of the commissioner and his deputies.

The building was so large that writers in 1891 estimated that ten to fifteen thousand immigrants could pass through in a single day. Furthermore, for such a functional place, it looked good in the harbor. Reporting on the construction, the *New York Times* praised its beauty and size: "When completed the building will be a handsome addition to the orna-

ments of the harbor. . . . An idea of the building's size is suggested by the fact that 4,000,000 feet of timber has been used in its construction."

That mass of timber was mainly Georgia pine, noteworthy for its strength and beauty—the interior walls were left unfinished to show it off. Wooden buildings hardly connoted permanence, however, and catastrophic fires were not unknown in wooden-walled buildings in the nineteenth century. One New York newspaper undertook an explanation in 1891:

It is in keeping with many other Government enterprises that the massive structure is built wholly of wood, and from the nature of the material used in construction, temporary in character. But judging from the constant and ever-increasing invasion of the foreign-born to these

The three-story building spanned more than 400 feet and was 150 feet wide. When constructed, the main building of Ellis Island was expected to easily handle ten thousand immigrants daily. (Photo courtesy of the Library of Congress)

The original main building on Ellis Island featured buff-painted wooden walls, picturesque turreted towers, and blue slate roofing. (Photo courtesy of the New York Historical Society)

It took just three hours for the four million board feet of Georgia pine in Ellis Island's turreted main building to burn to the ground on June 15, 1897. Because of the shallow channel around the island, fire-fighting tugboats could not get close enough to spray the buildings. All the immigrants and immigration personnel were evacuated safely, but most of the immigration records, dating back to 1855, were destroyed. (Photo courtesy of the National Archives)

shores, the Old World will probably be drained of its superfluous population before the building has outlived its usefulness. It was not, however, for this reason, but through an insufficiency of appropriation, that the building was constructed out of wood.

After numerous delays the island station opened on January 1, 1892. Three steamships, the *Nevada*, the *City of Paris*, and the *Victoria*, landed a total of seven hundred steerage passengers on that day of inauguration. The first immigrant to land and have her name placed at the top of the registration book was fifteen-year-old Annie Moore, from County Cork, Ireland. By prearrangement the Irish youngster was registered by Charles Hendley, the former private secretary to Treasury Secretary Windom. Following

that official business, Commissioner Weber welcomed Annie with a short speech and the presentation of a $10 gold piece. Ellis Island was officially open!

During the ensuing early years at Ellis Island officials had to adjust to new laws and new procedures, but their task was facilitated by a decline in immigration during the 1890s by one-third from the previous decade. A cholera scare in European ports in the fall of 1892 caused President Benjamin Harrison to raise quarantine standards at American ports, triggering the decline. Later, the financial panic of 1893 and the subsequent depression, which lasted through much of the decade, made the United States far less attractive to foreign workers.

The new routine adopted at Ellis Island and elsewhere was intended to make examinations more thorough. A new set of Treasury Department regulations

These Dutch children in their wooden sabots would have been a rare sight amid the newcomers of the 1890s, who were generally from southern and eastern Europe. They are holding their examination cards, indicating they have passed the Ellis Island inspection process. (Photo courtesy of the National Park Service)

Unnoticed among the 445,987 immigrants passing through Ellis Island in its first year (1892) was a four-year-old Russian named Israel Baline, who became known as Irving Berlin. This 1915 picture shows the young songwriter who had achieved international success with "Alexander's Ragtime Band" four years previously. Among Irving Berlin's fifteen hundred songs is "God Bless America," celebrating his new homeland, and the music for films such as Top Hat *(1935),* On the Avenue *(1937), and* Annie Get Your Gun *(1946). (Photo courtesy of the Bettmann Archive)*

Immigration officials were particularly concerned about the fate of female immigrants arriving alone at Ellis Island. Officials feared that, without the protection of a male relative or friend, the women might fall prey to unscrupulous elements. Consequently, neither this Lithuanian woman (left), if she came alone to Ellis Island, nor this Syrian mother and her children (below) would be released from Ellis Island until husbands or relatives came to pick them up. (Photo on the left by Lewis W. Hine, courtesy of the New York Public Library, and photo below courtesy of the National Park Service)

Under the new U.S. Treasury Department rules, shipping clerks, like these for the Hamburg-America Line, kept more detailed records on their immigrant passengers. The writing on the wall (background) reads, "My field is the world." (Photo courtesy of the National Archives)

issued in April 1893 required the shipping companies to keep more detailed records on their passengers. When these passengers were landed at immigration stations, they were to be accompanied by ships' manifests listing each person's name, age, sex, marital status, occupation, literacy, nationality, last residence, landing place and final destination in the United States, funding sources, money in possession, criminal record, relatives in the United States, previous visits to the United States, history of dependence on public support or work as a contract laborer, record of polygamy, and general health condition. Examiners at points of entry were to compare these records with information derived from their own verbal and physical examinations of the immigrants.

The new regulations also further clarified the deportation process. Immigrants who were found to fall within prohibited classes could appeal, in writing, directly to the Treasury Department. All cases in question were heard by an Ellis Island board of four (later three) inspectors. If the majority found against an immigrant's right to enter the country, the person could then appeal to the Treasury Department. While the appeal process took place, or while unsuccessful applicants awaited return to ports of origin, their expenses during their stay on the island were the responsibility of the shipping company that had brought them.

Also as a result of the Immigration Act of 1891, medical examinations were more thorough at Ellis Island than they had been at the crowded Barge Office. The law provided that these exams be supervised by the United States Marine Hospital Service, a federal civil service corps of physicians in the Treasury Department (which became the U.S. Public Health Service early in the twentieth century). An instruction manual issued by the service clarified procedures and classified immigrants by types of affliction. In Class A were persons suffering from dangerous or loathsome diseases, insane persons, and idiots. Commonly found dangerous diseases included trachoma, a highly communicable eye disease, and pulmonary tuberculosis. Loathsome diseases were favus, a contagious skin disease, and syphilis. Aliens in Class A were automatically excluded by the boards of special inquiry. Class B cases—aliens with hernias, poor physiques, deformities, and varicose veins, as well as all pregnant women—were not automatically excluded but were further examined because they might tend to become public charges. As federal laws concerning what manner of immigrant was admissible became more stringent in the 1890s, medical practices at the examining station changed.

While professionalism was apparent in the medical corps, some positions were filled in the old-fashioned way—through political connections. Early in the federal administration of Ellis Island, for example, Colonel Weber encountered one such political protégé in the position of superintendent of landing (a position later abolished as superfluous). When

An old woman awaits the arrival of some relative or friend. In nine cases out of ten, older people were detained on Ellis Island. Sometimes, according to one inspector, "these poor unfortunates would wander about, bewilderment and incomprehension in their eyes, not even knowing where they were or why they were being detained." (Photo by Lewis W. Hine, courtesy of the New York Public Library)

Weber inquired what office furniture the employee needed, he was informed that it did not matter, as long as a comfortable sofa and chair were included. When pressed by the commissioner as to the nature of the work he intended to do in the office, the underling replied: "I see from your manner that you and I had better come to an understanding of matters at once. This position with its salary has been given to me in payment for services already rendered."

Other patronage appointments had happier results. When the new Democratic president, Grover Cleveland, took office in March 1893, he appointed Dr. Joseph H. Senner as Colonel Weber's successor. The new commissioner of immigration was known chiefly as a writer for German-language newspapers in New York, but he had actively campaigned for the Cleveland ticket in 1892. According to one newspaper, Senner was regarded by Treasury Department officials "as peculiarly well fitted for the place, and free from local complications, both political and commercial." This assessment was borne out by other newspapers, by the Senate Committee on Immigration, and by Senner's subsequent performance in office.

"I remember we had good times, we had bad times, we had all kinds of things [but] that hope to be in America was so great that it colored all the pain that we had during our trip. Of course, there was lots of trouble and suffering but there was a light within, in the soul, that gave us courage to go on."
—Gertrude Yellin, emigrated from Russia in 1921

Despite Dr. Senner's competence, his administration was not without its problems. Even before he took office, the structural quality of the buildings at Ellis Island was questioned and became a matter of ongoing concern in both Washington and New York. The main building had been open for only five months when an inspector was dispatched by Congress to ascertain the truth of charges that the building was "in danger of falling down." He reported that needed repairs were so minor that "the most serious one discovered can be fully repaired at an expense of $4.50." Two architects later testified before Congress on the inadequacies of the construction, estimating that $150,000 would be required to resolve the deficiencies. The congressional investigating committee, unable to decide between the $4.50 and $150,000 estimates, mirrored the professional schizophrenia by submitting majority and minority reports, each favoring one plan or the other. Unable to figure out what to do, Congress did nothing, except occasionally dispatch another professional consultant.

Temperance groups also fomented problems for Ellis Island officials when they complained about the operation of saloons at the immigration station in 1895. The superintendent of immigration in Washington, Herbert Stump, explained the situation. He noted the absence of good-tasting water on the island and stated that the immigrants were dissatisfied with the soft drinks like ginger ale and sarsaparilla sold there. Thinking these drinks were American beer, they received a distasteful surprise. Since many of the immigrants were accustomed to beer and wine with their meals, the Immigration Bureau had decided there would be no harm in selling these nonspiritous drinks on the island. Stump denied the presence of a saloon, however, and noted that the temperance societies would perform a valuable service for the immigrants by wiping out "the vile dens of iniquity into which they are beguiled after leaving [Ellis Island]." (Stump's statement was synonymous, it would seem, with "mind your own business.")

A more serious criticism of the island's administration was the concern voiced in several quarters over the government's leasing arrangement with the restaurant operators and money changers on the island. As one writer explained, "The restaurant has the hungry immigrant absolutely at its mercy. It may sell mince pies made of dog meat and customers are bound to come. It may distribute soup wherein are mingled all things clean and unclean, and the procession of customers will constantly come and call for

Peering over the railing of the SS Baltic are women hoping to become brides. "Picture brides" often were imported for American men. The "marriageable girl" below is one of a thousand arriving on September 27, 1907. Occasionally a shipboard romance would dash the dreams of the waiting beau. However, most "brides" completed the voyage across the Atlantic still betrothed. (Photos courtesy of the Library of Congress)

▲
When the sponsoring person called for this Hungarian mother and children, he or she began at the Information Department, where an inspector made sure the sponsor was the correct person. If the name or previous history of the prospective immigrant was not in agreement with the inspector's information, the case went before the Special Inquiry Board. (Photo courtesy of the National Park Service)

◄ *The newcomers' transformation on Ellis Island was rapid. The woman in the background is carrying her baggage as she might in her native land, but the identification tag about her neck is the first sign of her Americanization. Before they left the island, many immigrants already had exchanged their Old World Sunday best for New World fashions brought by relatives and friends. (Photo by Lewis W. Hine, courtesy of the New York Public Library)*

Steamship companies were responsible for the cost of immigrants' meals while they were on Ellis Island. Breakfast was supposed to include bread and tea or coffee with milk and/or sugar. Dinner was to be soup, boiled meat (except Fridays, when fish was to be offered), and potatoes. But early restaurant contractors recognized the profit potential and substituted inadequate, cheaper meals. (Photo courtesy of the New York Public Library)

Efforts to ferret out corruption in the early years of the twentieth century did not overlook these food vendors. Menus were greatly improved and dining hall operations were closely monitored by 1926, when this photo was taken. (Photo by Lewis W. Hine, courtesy of the New York Public Library)

The money exchange offered ample opportunities for sting operators. Some could—with smooth sleight of hand—remove dollar bills from the immigrants' exchanged funds and pocket them. The man leaning into the line is probably cautioning his comrade. (Photo courtesy of the New York Public Library)

more." The steamship companies paid a fixed rate of 50¢ a day for each detained immigrant, an amount that was supposed to be sufficient to provide three meals a day consisting of bread, soup, and sausage. The actual fare was more modest, however, and seems to have been a steady source of profit for the restaurateurs.

The money exchange also provided ample opportunities for fraud. The *New York Times*, not usually given to crusades, found that the exclusive privilege offered to money changers had the potential for "one of the most wholesale bunko games ever perpetrated in this country." Furthermore, the *Times* railed against the whole process in the immigration station, in which the newly arrived aliens "had no more to say about the subsequent proceedings than a flock of sheep in the big Chicago Stock yards."

While these writers displayed a sympathetic interest in the welfare of the immigrants, numerous others focused instead on the problems the United States faced in attempting to assimilate the new wave of immigrants. The popular magazines of the 1890s frequently printed articles warning the general populace about the dangers of unrestricted immigration.

Meanwhile the immigrants kept coming, 110,000 more in 1896 than in the previous year, 77 percent of them through Ellis Island. A medical examiner who worked there compared the arrivals with "a circus procession plus a hustle and bustle lacking in the more deliberate circus parade. . . . Hour after hour,

ship load after ship load, day after day, the stream of human beings with its kaleidoscopic variations was then hurried along through Ellis Island by the equivalent of 'step lively' in every language of the earth. There were few old-time employees at Ellis Island who could not tell an immigrant to 'hurry up' in at least a dozen languages."

The constant prodding to "hurry up" and "step lively" must have seemed inhospitable to the thousands of immigrants who passed through the station. The procedure might have saved lives, however, in the early morning hours of June 15, 1897. A fire broke out in the main building shortly before midnight on June 14. Flames shooting out of the building were clearly visible in Manhattan, as was the shower of flaming embers catapulted into the air when the roof collapsed around 1:00 A.M. With nearly all the buildings on fire, the entire island "seemed one big blaze," according to observers nearby. In spite of the automatic sprinklers in the main building and numerous fireplugs equipped with hoses and nozzles, the wooden buildings were swiftly engulfed in flames. Due to the shallow channel around the island, fire-fighting tugs could not get close enough to spray the buildings. Estimates of property losses ran from $500,000 to $750,000.

Incredibly, given the swiftness with which the fire spread, no lives were lost. Thirty-one employees escaped, along with 199 immigrants, fifty-five of whom were in the hospital. The paddle wheeler *John*

As the demographics of the new immigrants changed and their numbers grew in the 1890s, there was a groundswell of concern about the influx of "peasant stock" like this Romanian immigrant. Restrictionists feared that the long history of oppression in their native lands would impair the new immigrants' ability to adjust to the mainstream of American culture. (Photo courtesy of the National Park Service)

Pogroms throughout Russia were more perilous for Russian Jews than was the voyage to America. Thousands, like this man, came at the end of the nineteenth century seeking America's promise of religious and political freedom. (Photo by Lewis W. Hine, courtesy of the New York Public Library)

Immigrant assimilation was eased by ethnic neighborhoods, where the customs of the Old World were adapted to the new country. In this photo a clam vendor is finding his wares popular fare on Mulberry Street, a New York area settled predominantly by Italians. (Photo courtesy of the Library of Congress)

G. Carlisle was tied up at the ferry slip, and crew members served as litter bearers to rescue the nonambulatory hospital patients. When the fire reached the beams supporting the covered passageway leading to the ferry slip, the tin roof was pushed down and patients were carried over the still-smoldering structure. Seventeen minutes from the time the fire was discovered, all the immigrants on the island were transferred safely to boats.

The cause of the fire was never determined. As to the advisability of erecting wooden structures in the first place, the *New York World* made the harshest comment: "If a private individual or corporation had put up huge buildings of inflammable pine on a little island in the bay, and had kept there as many as three thousand five hundred persons from all over the earth, public opinion would have risen in its might. But the U.S. Government did it."

In its short lifetime the immigration station at Ellis Island had proved so useful as to leave no doubt that it should be rebuilt. Commissioner Senner had his own ideas about the project, and they did not

include Georgia pine. He explained:

Every day as I left the island during the past four years I gave a farewell look at the buildings, for I expected to return the next day and find them all in ashes. I knew that in case of a big fire there would be no way to fight the flames, for the water supply was limited. The buildings should be of iron and brick, and constructed similar to a modern steamship, consisting of compartments, divided by steel doors, which could be closed at night or at a minute's notice.

Superintendent Stump accordingly advised the secretary of the Treasury that more landfill should be added to the island, bringing the total acreage to seventeen. The structures should include a main building, a hospital with staff quarters, and a restaurant and kitchen building. All buildings should be of fireproof construction (although he left out the steel-doored compartments), the cost of which he estimated at $600,000.

This was essentially the plan the government

The U.S. immigration staff poses during a quiet period, a rare occurrence at Ellis Island in the early years. Inspectors handling the flood tide of immigration at the turn of the twentieth century often worked long hours. It was not unusual for an inspector to be responsible for examining four to five hundred newcomers daily. (Photo courtesy of the YIVO Institute for Jewish Research)

Conditions at the Barge Office did not always put America's best foot forward. Two messengers were dismissed for taking payoffs, and a gateman was discharged for assaulting immigrants. By 1900, when this photo was taken, many of the Barge Office's abuses had been corrected. (Photo courtesy of the Byron Collection, Museum of the City of New York)

By April 2, 1900, when this photo was taken, fireproof construction of the new main building on Ellis Island was well under way. The wooden deck under what would eventually be a red-tiled roof is visible over the building's vaulted segment. (Photo courtesy of the National Archives)

By June 30, 1900, the decorative brick-and-limestone turrets were rising above the main entrance, and the main building was totally enclosed. The main building of Ellis Island was the first important government architecture that was awarded according to the design competition requirements of the Tarnsey Act of 1875. The Broadway firm of Boring & Tilton won the competition. (Photo courtesy of the National Archives)

The French Renaissance design period, of which Ellis Island is a premier example, featured intricate stonework detailing. Of particular architectural note are the filigree work in the spire-capped turrets and above the right wing's roofline. The exterior red-and-white decorative awnings add a finishing touch on the progressive first-floor Chicago-style windows. (Photo courtesy of the New York Public Library)

At a construction cost of approximately $1.5 million, the new immigration station was opened on December 17, 1900. After proceeding under the awning, the first immigrants went through their initial inspection in the main building. (Photo courtesy of the New York Public Library)

The old ferry building at the end of the slip stands in stark contrast to the ornate architecture of the new main building. (Photo courtesy of the National Archives)

adopted. The architectural competition for the buildings was won by the New York firm of Boring & Tilton in December 1897. In the subsequent four years the firm planned an overall layout of the island and designed the main building, a kitchen and restaurant building, a bathhouse and laundry building (with a connecting corridor), a powerhouse, and a hospital building with an adjacent surgeon's house. The hospital and surgeon's house were built on a strip of land created by new landfill located south of the ferry slip and the main building. In subsequent years this area was designated Island Number 2.

The main building was a handsome structure in a style usually referred to as French Renaissance. The central portion of the building contained a second-floor registry room two hundred feet long and one hundred feet wide with a high vaulted ceiling. At each corner of this central section was a tower clad with copper. A two-story wing at each end of the building completed the structure. The immigration building was constructed of brick over a steel frame and finished with limestone trim. The design was so impressive that a model was exhibited at the Trans-Mississippi Exposition at Omaha in 1898. One writer referred to it as a "handsome work of art" and likened it to the more aesthetic palaces of the Old World.

While awaiting the completion of this immigration palace, it was back to the Barge Office for 3½ years. All the old problems—overcrowding, lack of proper facilities, the confidence men and other predators—immediately reappeared. In addition, charges of mistreatment of immigrants and laxity in administration were lodged against Commissioner Thomas Fitchie, who had replaced Dr. Senner in 1897, and his assistant, Edward McSweeney. Political infighting among officials in Washington and New York led to an extensive hearing on conditions at the Barge Office. As a result of the investigation, two messengers were dismissed from service for taking money from friends of immigrants, and a gateman was discharged for his rough treatment of immigrants and the use of profane language.

Whenever writers or immigration officials discussed problems at the Barge Office in the late 1890s, they uniformly stated that these problems would disappear with the reopening of Ellis Island. The reopening took place on December 17, 1900, when 654 Italians from the *Kaiser Wilhelm II* landed at the island. Some of the problems, however, remained.

Passenger barges Wm. Fletcher *and* John E. Moore *rest at dock in front of the completed main building. The reopening of Ellis Island was expected to signal a new beginning in immigration procedures. However, some problems remained, and new ones would develop. (Photo by A. Loeffler, courtesy of the Library of Congress)*

FOUR

The Rise of Anti-Immigration Sentiment

In the mid–nineteenth century, as America's population grew in number and diversity, immigration became an increasingly controversial issue. Some Americans grew concerned about the vast numbers of Catholics entering the country from Ireland and Germany. Prominent among concerned citizens was famed inventor Samuel F. B. Morse, who wrote articles and books decrying "foreign designs through the Roman Catholic religion." He and others urged that suffrage be withheld from all immigrants. As a New Brunswick, New Jersey, man commented in 1850, "The simple truth is that the honest men of the country are tired of being voted down by the . . . foreigners in this city, a vast majority of whom were ten years ago the ignorant serfs of Ireland."

Such feelings gave rise to an antebellum nativist movement, expressed through the formation of numerous local anti-Catholic and anti-immigrant societies. These nativists formed a political party to promote their views—the American Party, popularly known as the Know-Nothing Party. The party advocated the election of native-born Americans to public office, more stringent naturalization legislation, and curtailing immigration. The party's influence peaked in 1855 when it controlled 48 seats in Congress but dissolved rapidly under the onslaught of a growing sectionalism prior to the Civil War.

The Civil War proved a breakwater not only to the first wave of immigration but also to the growing nativist (or anti-immigrant) movement. After the war immigration recovered its momentum faster than the nativist movement, primarily because most Americans were too busy picking up the pieces or starting over on the frontier to pay close heed to the immigrants entering the country.

◀ *America's Lady of the Harbor appears to be ignoring these detained but determined immigrants. Ellis Island could be a rampart of jubilant hope or a landfill of quiet desperation. (Photo courtesy of the Theodore Koch Collection, Michigan Historical Collections, Bentley Historical Library, University of Michigan)*

However, the 1890s saw a groundswell in the nativist movement. The resurgent nativism derived from several sources. First, in 1890 the U.S. Census Bureau announced that there was no longer an American frontier. No longer were there thousands of unclaimed acres to help absorb the millions fleeing a war-ridden, overcrowded Europe. Second, American laborers grew increasingly concerned about losing jobs to the vast numbers of immigrants who were willing to work for lower wages and longer hours—a concern exacerbated by the depression of the mid-1890s.

The fears of nativists were not restricted to the number of immigrants but focused as well on their character and origins. Unlike their predecessors, the newcomers of the 1890s were drawn increasingly from southern and eastern Europe—Italians, Poles, Slavs, and Russian Jews. Many came from countries with strong monarchies. Many were Catholic. Most spoke unfamiliar languages. Many were unskilled, many uneducated.

Magazine and newspaper journalists joined some politicians and intellectuals in railing against the admission of millions of these people. A typical argument for restriction was made by Nathaniel Shaler in an 1893 *Atlantic Monthly* article entitled "European Peasants as Immigrants." Shaler described the mass of American immigrants as originating in the peasant stock of Europe, a class that had, over centuries, lost all ambition for political and social equality. A few years later a writer in *Century Magazine*, while conceding that the question of immigration restriction was multifaceted, concluded, "When one sees the mass of low cosmopolitan humanity such as is to be found at Ellis Island, one cannot help feeling that to assimilate it the country has need of an excellent digestion."

The nativist movement garnered enough popular support to give it political clout. The Populist party, an agrarian-based political conglomeration

This seven-member family shared a one-room efficiency apartment for all activities, including eating and sleeping. Because the inability to read was linked to the United States' growing ghettos, the proposed Immigration Bill of 1897 included a literacy test. (Photo by Jacob Riis, courtesy of the Museum of the City of New York)

The new immigrants often were willing to work for pennies, which injured the earning potential of more established American workers and led to the proliferation of "sweatshops." Piecework abounded, and there were no child—or family pet—labor laws, so all family members contributed to earning their daily bread. (Photo by Jacob Riis, courtesy of the Museum of the City of New York)

with strong bases in the South and Midwest, featured immigration restriction in its national platform of 1896. Groups such as the American Protective Association (mainly anti-Catholic) and the Boston-based Immigration Restriction League actively sought ways to shut the door to would-be immigrants. These groups and others like them helped to sponsor legislation that included the imposition of a literacy test as part of the standard examination of steerage passengers.

Under the leadership of U.S. Senator Henry Cabot Lodge, the Immigration Bill of 1897, which among other things included a literacy test, passed both houses of Congress before President Grover Cleveland vetoed it. The veto proved to be only a temporary setback, however. The nativists continued to lobby, and they eventually secured both a literacy test (1917) and a quota system (1921).

Although the social, economic, and political conditions changed in favor of the nativists, the arguments for and against restricting immigration remained basically the same and are most eloquently stated in the debate between Senator Lodge and President Cleveland before the 55th Congress.

Anti-immigration factions sought to restrict immigrants of eastern European peasant stock, like this Serbian family from Yugoslavia, because it was felt they would "pollute the young nation's bloodline." (Photo courtesy of the National Park Service)

A labor agency on New York City's lower West Side advertises jobs in coal mines, with the railroads, and on construction sites paying from $2.20 to $3.55 per day. Although these jobs required little skill, they were often dangerous. American workers were reluctant to take the risks, so the jobs went to immigrants eager to establish themselves in their new homeland. (Photo by Lewis W. Hine, courtesy of the New York Public Library)

This photo of Mulberry Street in lower Manhattan depicts the congested and frantic lifestyle of the street vendors and ▶ pushcart peddlers in a predominantly ethnic enclave. Appalled by the crowded neighborhoods, restrictionists overlooked the fact that, if they could not find jobs, the new immigrants often created their own livelihoods. (Photo by Jacob Riis, courtesy of the Museum of the City of New York)

Here is Henry Cabot Lodge speaking before the United States Senate on March 16, 1896, in favor of the Immigration Bill of 1897, which included a literacy test as a standard for admission:

"Mr. President, this bill is intended to amend the existing law so as to restrict still further immigration to the United States. . . .

"The illiteracy test will bear most heavily upon the Italians, Russians, Poles, Hungarians, Greeks, and Asiatics, and very lightly, or not at all, upon English-speaking emigrants or Germans, Scandinavians, and French. In other words, the races most affected by the illiteracy test are those whose emigration to this country has begun within the last twenty years and swelled rapidly to enormous proportions, races with which the English-speaking people have never hitherto assimilated, and who are most alien to the great body of the people of the United States. . . .

"The statistics prepared by the committee [on immigration] show further that the immigrants excluded by the illiteracy test are those who remain for the most part in congested masses in our great cities. They furnish a large proportion of the population of the slums. The committee's report proves that illiteracy runs parallel with the slum population, with criminals, paupers, and juvenile delinquents of foreign birth or parentage, whose percentage is out of all proportion to their share of the total population when compared with the percentage of the same classes among the native born. . . .

"These facts prove to demonstrate that the exclusion of immigrants unable to read or write, as proposed by this bill, will operate against the most undesirable and harmful part of our present immigration and shut out elements which no thoughtful or patriotic man can wish to see multiplied among the people of the United States. . . .

"There is no one thing which does so much to bring about a reduction of wages and to injure the American wage earner as the unlimited introduction of cheap foreign labor through unrestricted immigration. Statistics show that the change in the race character of our immigration has been accompanied by a corresponding decline in its quality. . . .

"Russians, Hungarians, Poles, Bohemians, Italians, Greeks, and even Asiatics, whose immigration to America was almost unknown twenty years ago, have during the last twenty years poured in, in stead-

ily increasing numbers, until now they nearly equal the immigration of those races kindred in blood or speech, or both, by whom the United States has hitherto been built up and the American people formed.

"This momentous fact is the one which confronts us today, and if continued, it carries with it future consequences far deeper than any other event of our times. . . .

"Mr. President, more precious even than forms of government are the mental and moral qualities which make what we call our race. While those stand unimpaired all is safe. When those decline all is imperiled. They are exposed to but a single danger, and that is by changing the quality of our race and citizenship through the wholesale infusion of races whose traditions and inheritances, whose thoughts and whose beliefs are wholly alien to ours and with whom we have never assimilated or even been associated in the past, the danger has begun. . . .

"In careless strength, with generous hand, we have kept our gates wide open to all the world. If we do not close them, we should at least place sentinels beside them to challenge those who would pass through. The gates which admit men to the United States and to citizenship in the great Republic should no longer be left unguarded."

An Italian worker on New York State's Barge Canal reads the evening paper in the bunkhouse. Senator Lodge considered this immigrant among the "foreign labor which . . . not only takes lower wages, but accepts a standard of life and living so low that the American workingman can not compete with it." (Photo by Lewis W. Hine, courtesy of the New York Public Library)

These threshers near Grafton, North Dakota, gave credence to President Cleveland's view of immigration. Cleveland felt the United States' growth relied on "the assimilation and thrift of millions of sturdy and patriotic adopted citizens." (Photo courtesy of the Minnesota Historical Society)

President Grover Cleveland vetoed the bill, and on March 2, 1897, he repudiated Senator Lodge's arguments in a message to Congress that Americans may read with pride:

"I herewith return, without approval, House bill numbered 7864, entitled 'An Act to Amend the Immigration Laws of the United States. . . .'

"A radical departure from our national policy relating to immigration is here presented. Heretofore we have welcomed all who came to us from other lands, except those whose moral or physical condition or history threatened danger to our national welfare and safety. Relying upon the jealous watchfulness of our people to prevent injury to our political and social fabric, we have encouraged those coming from foreign countries to cast their lot with us and join in the development of our vast domain, securing in return a share in the blessings of American citizenship.

"A century's stupendous growth, largely due to the assimilation and thrift of millions of sturdy and patriotic adopted citizens, attests the success of this generous and freehanded policy, which, while guarding the people's interests, exacts from our immigrants only physical and moral soundness and a willingness and ability to work.

"It is said, however, that the quality of recent immigration is undesirable. The time is quite within recent memory when the same thing was said of immigrants who, with their descendants, are now numbered among our best citizens.

"The claim is also made that the influx of foreign laborers deprives of the opportunity to work those who are better entitled than they to the privilege of earning their livelihood by daily toil. An unfortunate condition is certainly presented when any who are willing to labor are unemployed. But so far as this condition now exists among our people, it must be conceded to be a result of phenomenal business depression and the stagnation of all enterprises in which labor is a factor.

"It is proposed by the bill under consideration to meet the alleged difficulties of the situation by establishing an educational test by which the right of a foreigner to make his home with us shall be determined. Its general scheme is to prohibit from admission to our country all immigrants 'physically capable and over sixteen years of age who can not read and write the English language or some other language'; and it is provided that this test shall be applied by requiring immigrants seeking admission to read and afterwards to write not less than twenty nor more than twenty-five words of the Constitution of the United States in some language, and that any immigrant failing in this shall not be admitted, but shall be returned to the country from whence he came at the expense of the steamship or railroad company which brought him.

"The best reason that could be given for this radical restriction of immigration is the necessity of protecting our population against degeneration and saving our national peace and quiet from imported turbulence and disorder.

"I can not believe that we would be protected against these evils by limiting immigration to those who can read and write in any language twenty-five words of our Constitution. In my opinion it is infinitely more safe to admit a hundred thousand immigrants who, though unable to read and write, seek among us only a home and opportunity to work, than to admit one of those unruly agitators and enemies of governmental control, who can not only read and write but delights in arousing by inflammatory speech the illiterate and peacefully inclined to discontent and tumult."

President Cleveland refuted Senator Lodge's arguments, saying, "Heretofore we have welcomed all who came to us from other lands. . . ." And immigrants were welcomed. At times so many were welcomed that they were forced to eat in shifts at Ellis Island. (Photo courtesy of the Theodore Koch Collection, Michigan Historical Collections, Bentley Historical Library, University of Michigan)

Carefully etching an ornate bronze corner molding, an Italian artisan belies Senator Lodge's fear of sharing America with "low, unskilled, ignorant, foreign labor." (Photo by Lewis W. Hine, courtesy of the New York Public Library)

Immigrant families were willing to earn their wages in whatever ways were open to them. This new resident of the United States prepares to board his bike and deliver the Western Union telegram tucked into his jacket pocket. (Photo by Jacob Riis, courtesy of the Museum of the City of New York)

Encouraged by their parents, immigrant children often were taught American customs by business-owned schools, such as the Mott Street Industrial School. Here they are learning to salute the flag of their adopted country. (Photo by Jacob Riis, courtesy of the Museum of the City of New York)

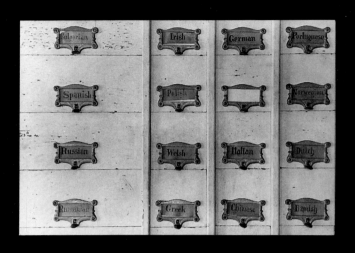

FIVE

The Flood Tide of Immigration, 1900–1917

One of the great migrations in the history of the world took place between 1900 and 1914. More than thirteen million people emigrated to the United States from abroad. In six of those years more than a million entered; in four other years the count was more than eight hundred thousand. After 1901 more immigrants came in each year than in any entire decade prior to the first great wave of the 1840s.

More than 75 percent of these newcomers passed through the Port of New York. This presented a serious problem at Ellis Island. All the optimism of the late 1890s about the spaciousness and grandeur of the new examining station had been based on earlier figures. Most analysts assumed that the great wave of immigration had spent itself in the 1880s and early 1890s. Consequently the facilities the government built were simply not adequate for the great tide of immigrants that began at the turn of the century. What had been portrayed as a magnificent example of government planning was obsolete practically by the day it opened.

Erecting buildings, then filling in land, then erecting more buildings characterized the physical and structural evolution of Ellis Island before World War I. When the island reopened in December 1900, the main building, the power house, and the laundry building constituted the facilities. A hospital and laundry across the ferry slip, on Island Number 2, opened in 1902. A railroad ticket office was added to the rear (on the north side) of the main building in 1904.

In 1906, due to complaints from the Public Health Service about the inefficiency of transporting diseased immigrants to Ward's Island, a new landfill operation created Island Number 3, linked to the other islands by a narrow causeway. (Ellis Island became, in reality, three islands linked by causeways.) A group of sixteen buildings, with connecting corridors, designed to lodge aliens with contagious diseases (a separate building for each disease) was completed on Island Number 3 in 1909. The original hospital, on Island Number 2, proved insufficient for the heavy traffic after 1902, and a hospital extension, separated from the original hospital building by an administration building, opened in 1908.

A baggage and dormitory building of two stories was erected adjacent (and connected by a corridor) to the railroad ticket office in 1908. Even that proved insufficient, and a third story was added five years after the original construction. A third story was added to the west wing of the main building in 1911 and to the east wing three years later. To the babel of tongues that entered the registration building with each shipload of immigrants was added the almost constant din of construction work before World War I.

Not all of the problems at Ellis Island related to overcrowding. Politics also intervened. Terence Powderly, former head of the Knights of Labor, had been appointed commissioner general (a title that supplanted the earlier superintendent) of immigration in 1897, for services rendered in William McKinley's successful presidential campaign of 1896. Powderly remained a partisan in political matters and directed New York commissioner Thomas Fitchie and his assistant, Edward McSweeney, to act in the same fashion. When Powderly and McSweeney had a falling-out, major political repercussions resulted in various charges being lodged against the administration of Ellis Island. Fueled by New York newspaper reports, new scandals broke in 1901, and charges of fraud and ineptitude once again erupted against the Fitchie administration.

◀ *These drawers in the library were labeled by nationality. The labels indicated not only the language of the literature behind them but also the diverse origins of the flood tide of humanity that crested on America's shores at the turn of the twentieth century. (Photo by Wilton S. Tifft)*

An Italian mother and child sit quietly outside a detention room, waiting for their loved ones. The detention cells were designed to hold six hundred people. During the early 1900s, however, Ellis Island was handling more than ninety thousand arrivals monthly. Often nine hundred newcomers were squeezed into a room; sometimes up to seventeen hundred people were pressed together. (Photo by Lewis W. Hine, courtesy of the New York Public Library)

Of the five thousand immigrants who arrived daily in 1905, about 20 percent spent their first night on Ellis Island. The complex had almost two hundred collapsible, three-tiered iron bedsteads. However, like the young eastern European above, many people, had to improvise. Benches, chairs, and floors were temporarily transformed into practical, albeit less comfortable, sleeping quarters. (Photo by Lewis W. Hine, courtesy of the New York Public Library)

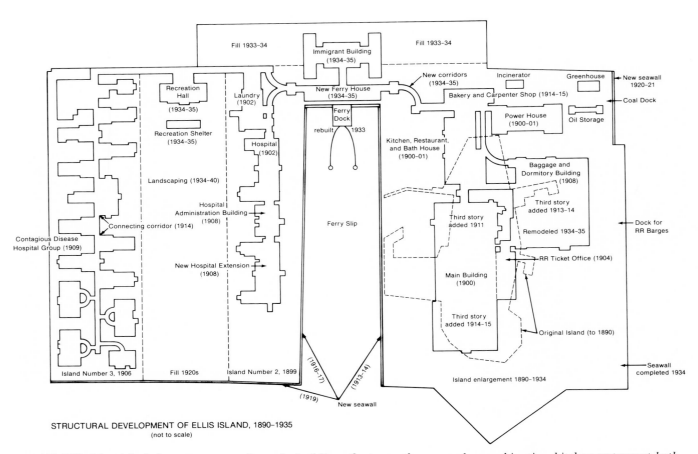

STRUCTURAL DEVELOPMENT OF ELLIS ISLAND, 1890–1935
(not to scale)

In 1900 Ellis Island had three structures: the main building, the power house, and a combination kitchen-restaurant-bath-house building. But even before the new facilities opened, the government realized they were woefully inadequate to handle the number of immigrants and began planning for expansion. By 1909 Ellis Island had grown into more than twenty buildings on three islands—the main complex on Island Number 1, the hospital facilities on Island Number 2, and the contagious diseases quarantine area on the third island, which was connected to Island Number 2 by a narrow causeway. (Illustration by Rosemary Morrissey-Herzberg)

Looking across the ferry slip from the main building, immigrants of the early 1900s faced an imposing hospital and medical administration complex (right foreground). The two-story house (left foreground) was used as the surgeon's residence. Isolated by a narrow ferry slip behind the hospital complex, some of the contagious diseases buildings (left background) also can be seen. (Photo courtesy of the New York Public Library)

On a rainy September day in 1903, Commissioner William Williams (right) welcomes an obviously pleased President Theodore Roosevelt (second from right). Williams's reform of the immigration station is considered one of the Roosevelt administration's success stories. (Photo courtesy of the New York Public Library)

By 1905 Ellis Island offered immigrants free meals but not organized entertainment. The overhead sign declares, "No charge for meals here" in six languages. The newcomers' esprit de corps, however, needed only an accordion to translate one man's music into another couple's dance. (Photo by Lewis W. Hine, courtesy of the New York Public Library)

On September 14, 1901, Theodore Roosevelt assumed the presidency after McKinley was assassinated by anarchist Leon Czolgosz. Roosevelt's interest in Ellis Island focused not only on setting in place a tough administration that would apply immigration laws fairly "in the interest of all for a higher grade of our common citizenship" but also on eliminating fraud and corruption. To achieve this he dismissed Powderly, Fitchie, and McSweeney in 1902. He selected as commissioner general another representative of organized labor, Frank P. Sargent, vice grand master of the Brotherhood of Locomotive Firemen. Fitchie's replacement was William Williams, a young Wall Street lawyer with a reputation for probity and, of special interest to Theodore Roosevelt, a sterling record in the Spanish-American War.

Like others, Roosevelt's stance on immigration had changed over the years. He had congratulated James Bryce, author of *The American Commonwealth*, for his understanding of the fact that "instead of the old American stock being 'swamped' by immigration, it has absorbed the immigrants and remained nearly unchanged." Yet Roosevelt was troubled by the new immigration of the 1890s. "I am very glad the immigration has come to a standstill for the last year," he wrote a friend in 1894. "We are

getting some very undesirable elements now, and I wish that a check could be put to it." He definitely favored the immigration restriction plans advanced by his friend and political ally, Senator Lodge.

Williams swept into office on April 28, 1902, determined to bring honesty and efficiency to the administration of the immigration station. His earliest concerns related to the fair treatment of immigrants, and one of his first decisive acts was to post the following notice over his name in public buildings on the island:

Immigrants must be treated with kindness and consideration. Any Government official violating the terms of this notice will be recommended for dismissal from the Service. Any other person so doing will be forthwith required to leave Ellis Island. It is earnestly requested that any violation hereof, or any instance of any kind of improper treatment of immigrants at Ellis Island, or before they leave the Barge Office, be promptly brought to the attention of the Commissioner.

Williams also instituted a number of administrative changes in the interest of efficiency. His concern was not only to detain all immigrants whose status

The Progressive Era of social and political reform coincided with the flood tide of immigration and brought humanizing changes to the process. Although Commissioner Williams adamantly followed the letter of the law, he also strongly believed the healthy family, like this Finnish clan, that stayed together passed through Ellis Island together. (Photo courtesy of the National Park Service)

Fifty-year-old Mary Johnson of Canada managed to pass through Ellis Island on October 4, 1908, as SS New York passenger "Frank Woodhull" even though Commissioner Williams had raised the standards for visual, mental, and physical inspections. For fifteen of the thirty years she lived in the United States she retained her masculine disguise. (Photo courtesy of the National Park Service)

was questionable but also to speed the flow of legal immigrants through the island to their destinations. He made clear his intention not to be saddled with political appointees or inefficient civil servants.

Williams was as meticulous about sanitary conditions as he was about administrative matters. His efforts evidently met with success. When Ernest Hamlin Abbott, one of the publishers of *The Outlook*, traveled to Ellis Island late in 1902, he observed, "The first impression which every visitor to Ellis Island must receive is of the surprising cleanliness and good ventilation . . . the floors [in the main building]—apparently of concrete—are washed from two to five times a day."

In spite of receiving praise for his efforts, the commissioner himself was more cautious. He noted, in an annual report, that "it is inconceivable that the millennium can ever exist here." This lack of perfection was owing to "the vastness of the work, the ignorance of the people with whom we deal, the large number of employees, and the temptations to which they are subjected."

Other observers agreed that the Williams admin-

istration indeed fell short of perfection and called for an investigation of alleged mistreatment of aliens on the island. Following a personal visit to the facility in 1903, President Roosevelt appointed a five-man commission to investigate the charges. After visiting the island and compiling hundreds of pages of testimony, the commission thoroughly exonerated Williams and made several recommendations to lighten the burden at Ellis Island. (These recommendations included construction of new facilities and the appointment of immigration inspectors at foreign ports, both of which Williams had already urged.)

Williams remained in office until January 1905, when he resigned to return to his law practice. He was succeeded by the able Robert Watchorn, a former United Mine Workers official who had been in the immigration service for a decade. (He had come to America via steerage from England in 1880, passing through Castle Garden. His most lasting memory of the ordeal was his pummeling of a vendor who had harassed him there.) Watchorn, like Williams, contended with political appointees and corrupt and inefficient food vendors, money changers, and bag-

Relatives and friends milled around the Barge Office, waiting to greet America's newest arrivals or to testify on behalf of a detained relative or friend on Ellis Island. The ferryboat ride between Ellis Island and the Barge Office ran every thirty minutes, on the hour and half hour. To board the ferryboat the crowd of mixed nationalities had to obtain passes from the steamship office. (Photo courtesy of the Theodore Koch Collection, Michigan Historical Collections, Bentley Historical Library, University of Michigan)

Tired immigrants often stood in seemingly endless lines before passing through the registry. Commissioner Robert Watchorn, who had entered America via steerage from England twenty-five years earlier, had benches installed along the aisles in the registry room between 1905 and 1909. (Photo by Lewis W. Hine, courtesy of the New York Public Library)

Commissioner Robert Watchorn (right) and an assistant flank a Russian giant (doorway in the background is 7½ feet high). A confirmed humanitarian, Watchorn often championed immigrant rights, even off Ellis Island. For example, when he learned that immigrants were being overcharged and undertreated as railroad passengers, Watchorn sent an inspector undercover to investigate and filed a complaint against the railroad with the Interstate Commerce Commission. (Photo courtesy of the National Park Service)

Escalating conflicts between the Russian aristocracy and the peasantry would culminate in the 1917 Revolution. In the meantime, thousands of Russians like these eight orphaned children, whose mothers were massacred in October 1900, sought refuge in America. (Photo courtesy of the National Park Service)

gage handlers who contracted for their exclusive concessions with the federal government. He was praised widely for his honesty, efficiency, and humane qualities in office. An example of his kindness was his decision to place benches along the aisles in the registry room, where tired immigrants often stood in line for hours awaiting examination. Watchorn also concerned himself with the fate of the immigrants after they left the island. Feeling that the railroad companies charged excessive rates to the newcomers and treated them as inferior passengers, he sent inspector Philip Cowan, disguised as an immigrant, on a train full of newly arrived aliens. When Cowan's findings confirmed his suspicions, Watchorn filed a complaint against the railroad with the Interstate Commerce Commission.

When William Howard Taft became president in 1909, he reappointed William Williams as commissioner at Ellis Island. In his second tour of duty Williams remained concerned about the civil and humane treatment of immigrants, posting a notice to all employees similar to the one he had written on assuming office in 1902. Williams continued his quest for efficient administration and cleanliness. He also designed a postcard to be sent to friends and relatives of detained immigrants, the "Notice to Call on Behalf of Detained Alien." The information on the card included the name and ship of the alien. The message read: "This alien refers to you. If you desire to call on his or her behalf, you may do so. Ferryboat leaves Barge Office (Battery Park), every half hour, on the hour. You are not required to pay anything to any one in connection with this matter."

The hallmark of the second Williams administration, however, was a concern for the restriction of unqualified immigrants. This new emphasis may have been based on numbers. In Williams's last year of his first term as commissioner (1904), 606,019 immigrants had come through Ellis Island. But the peak year was 1907, when 1,004,756 immigrants landed in New York, with an additional quarter of a million entering other ports in the United States. With so many more immigrants to process, Williams determined that "it is necessary that the standard of inspection at Ellis Island be raised." This meant informing prospective immigrants abroad of the high standard of immigration laws and the more effective

Little things meant a lot. Here immigrants (foreground) and inspectors (background) pause to celebrate Christmas 1906 on the balcony overlooking the registry room. Gifts from the Ellis Island staff included cards and apples. (Photo courtesy of the State Historical Society of Wisconsin)

training of the Ellis Island staff "in the exercise of proper care."

Williams paid particular attention to the exclusion of "paupers" and persons "likely to become a public charge," classes that had been examined leniently in the past. He quite simply set his own standard to determine such cases. "In the absence of a statutory provision," he mandated, "no hard and fast rule can be laid down as to the amount of money an immigrant must bring with him, but in most cases it will be unsafe for immigrants to arrive with less than twenty-five dollars ($25) besides railroad ticket to destination, while in many instances they should have more." Controversy erupted over the capricious nature of this proviso. The *New York Call* claimed it caused a "great deal of suffering" among the immigrants and pointed out that record numbers of applicants were being refused entry. The *Call* sensationalized the plight of those detained in its headline "Six

In 1917 New York Bible Society missionaries posed with some of the souls they had found in the baggage and dormitory building. Immigrants requesting "The Good Book" were given copies before embarking on their American journey. (Photo by A. F. Sherman courtesy of the National Geographic *magazine)*

Many religious and charitable organizations were on hand to offer guidance and support to immigrants on Ellis Island. Salvation Army soldiers marched among the Ellis Island entrants, providing breakfast doughnuts and moral support. (Photo courtesy of the Bettmann Archive)

Local groups also helped immigrants adjust to their new neighbors. The 1910 singing class at Hull House in Chicago was typical of the friendly and constructive interweaving of the new citizenry with their more established neighbors. (Photo by Lewis W. Hine, courtesy of the New York Public Library)

Urban settlement houses acclimated new arrivals to the American environment. Sympathetic workers taught English reading, writing, and speech and offered assistance in the naturalization process. The houses also might have provided recreational facilities, such as this backyard playground being put to good use by Bostonian children in 1912. (Photo by Lewis W. Hine, courtesy of the New York Public Library)

Hundred More Shut in 'Black Hole of Ellis Island' for Lack of $25."

In some of his recommendations for deportation Williams demonstrated a tough attitude. Addressing the commissioner general about the case of an Austrian woman who left at home four children and a husband with "swollen legs" and "weak eyes," Williams recommended exclusion. If she were allowed to land, he wrote, "the sick husband and four younger children would present themselves shortly for admission, and if we denied it sentimentalists would charge us with having *separated a family*. The way to keep this family from being separated is to send the woman back to her husband and children, with whom she belongs." In another case he argued against the admission of a deaf-mute girl of seven, coming to join her parents, who had been in the United States for three years. Williams wrote, "There is no reason why we should admit deaf and dumb children to this country whose parents cared so little for them in the past that they have left them in the care of others for three years."

Given the nature of the work, all administrations at Ellis Island engendered attacks, and the second Williams administration was no exception. In May 1911 Congressman William Sulzer called for an investigation into the "cruelty to helpless and unprotected immigrants" and "arbitrary and unnecessarily harsh methods" at Ellis Island. After taking statements from witnesses critical of Williams and from Williams himself, the House Committee on Rules dropped the investigation. Williams closed out his term in office strictly interpreting the immigration laws but also strictly safeguarding the interests of immigrants. Before leaving his post, he redrafted the rules and redefined the organization of the immigration service at Ellis Island.

"I used to go and look at this beautiful, fantastic building that, as we were arriving, looked like a palace and inside looked like a bare jail. . . . You had to wait in line to get the food. You had to get in line to get a blanket. . . . They weren't unkind, but they had so many people to take care of."
—*Barbara Barondess, emigrated from Russia in 1921*

Watchorn and Williams both reflected the spirit of the times during their tenure in office. The Williams and Watchorn administrations at Ellis Island came during a period not only of intensive immigration but also of intensive concern with domestic problems and their solutions. What historians call the "progressive era," from the turn of the century to World War I, was marked, among other things, by a thirst for social justice (for groups like immigrants, the impoverished, and women and children in industry) and a quest for efficiency in the administration of governmental agencies and private businesses.

Ethnic, religious, and charitable groups had long been a presence at the immigration station, dating back to the days at Castle Garden. At Ellis Island such groups were given office space and access to the incoming aliens. A 1905 magazine article by a member of the U.S. Public Health Service described the variety of services the groups offered:

They provide temporary shelter and protection for discharged aliens, and direct them to legitimate employers of labor. In this way they relieve the government of caring for many temporarily detained aliens, especially young women traveling alone. They write letters and send telegrams to the friends of the detained immigrants, and assist them in many other ways.

Many groups and individuals also decried the plight of the immigrants after they left Ellis Island. Charitable societies and aid societies for women and children increased their activities to assist in the assimilation of the newcomers. Settlement houses, which were instituted in American cities in the 1890s, established the presence of sympathetic Americans in urban immigrant neighborhoods. Settlement house

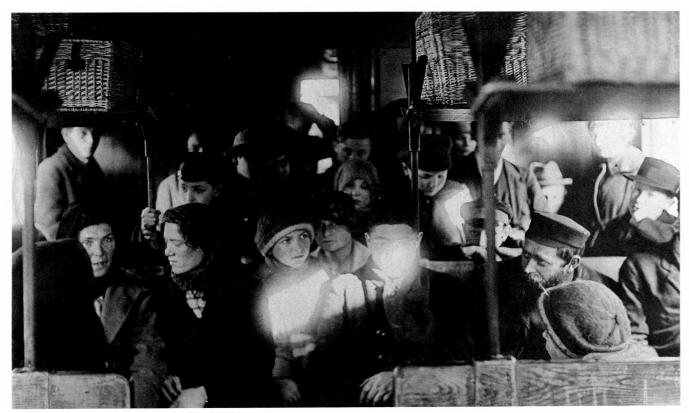

Potential immigrants were screened by steamship company agents before they could book passage to America. Agents in inland cities were held accountable for selling tickets to people who were later judged unfit by immigration inspectors. Having passed the initial screening, these Polish immigrants ride a passenger train to Gdansk on their way to America. (Photo courtesy of the YIVO Institute for Jewish Research)

The steamship company was liable for the return passage of those denied entry and could be fined $100 for each alien carrying a communicable disease. Therefore, candidates for immigration underwent a second scrutiny at the debarkation port. The Baltic America Line's emigrant house even featured a disinfection chamber for the immigrants' clothing. (Photo courtesy of the National Archives)

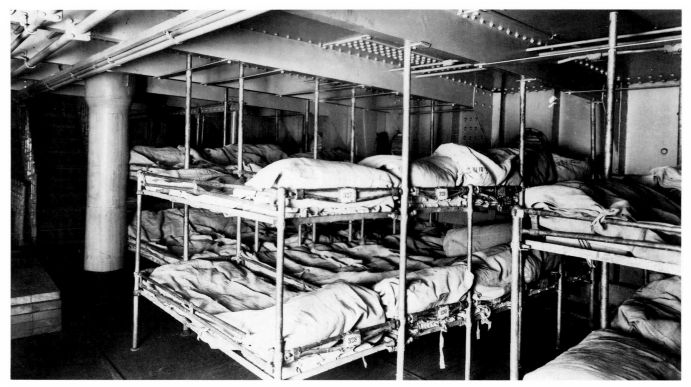

This corner angle of the below-deck steerage accommodations shows some of the three hundred or so iron-framed beds. When steerage was full, each passenger's space was limited to his or her straw-filled mattress, which may have featured a coarsely woven canvas slipcover but generally no pillows for weary heads. (Photo courtesy of the Byron Collection, the Museum of the City of New York)

Passenger names were recorded on the steamship's manifest, along with pertinent health, legal, and economic data. To resolve identification problems later, each arriving immigrant received cards (see photo on page 86) with a number printed on it. The number corresponded to the manifest page where information on that immigrant could be found. (Photo © Ernst Haas, courtesy of Magnum Photos, Inc.)

With passport or travel visa and manifest tag in hand, immigrants were ready to queue up for processing on Ellis Island. (Photo courtesy of the Library of Congress)

workers helped acculturate the immigrants by teaching them to read, write, and speak English; assisted them in the naturalization process; and provided recreational and educational facilities for immigrant children.

This flurry of interest in immigrants attracted writers to the subject. The more adventurous of them dressed up as immigrants and traveled in steerage to Ellis Island to observe the process firsthand and duly record it. Along with the reminiscences of the immigrants themselves, some of whom became famous or educated or both, these writings comprise an informative testimony about the hopes, fears, and experiences of the Europeans who transplanted themselves to America in the early twentieth century.

The immigration process began across the Atlantic, often with a pair of inspections by representatives of the steamship companies. The agents in the inland cities of Europe were held responsible by many of the companies if they sold tickets to immigrants who were later found unfit by immigration inspectors in America. Therefore they screened prospective buyers and refused passage to any they considered defective. Next came the examination at the port of debarkation. Because it was definitely in the interests of the steamship companies to exercise caution, their officials carefully scrutinized prospective passengers again. Not only was a company liable for the return passage of those denied entry, but Commissioner Williams assessed a $100 fine to any steamship company

Between 1901 and 1910 Ellis Island welcomed nearly seven million immigrants, roughly the number of people who now inhabit the five boroughs of New York City. In 1907 alone more than one million people were processed. During that same year, Ellis Island inspectors boarded 8,818 ships teeming with those who wanted to call America home. Nowhere was this massive influx of humanity more apparent than on the decks of the waiting steamships when, in good weather, the steerage passengers turned out for fresh air and exercise. (Photo courtesy of the Library of Congress)

The Immigration Service had a number of barges to ferry aliens, like this Italian family, from the pier or the ship to Ellis Island. Because eighty to one hundred thousand newcomers were arriving monthly during the height of immigration, it was not unusual for arrivals to spend several days and nights aboard the steamship before the barge could take them to the island. (Photo by Lewis W. Hine, courtesy of the New York Public Library)

that transported an alien with a communicable disease, which might be transmitted to others during the voyage.

On manifest sheets the steamship companies recorded the names of all passengers along with the answers to a list of required questions about health, legal, and financial status. In addition to the questions asked of immigrants in the 1890s, a new query was posed: was the passenger an anarchist? Inspired by President McKinley's assassination, an act of Congress in March 1903 had added this category for exclusion. Just to make sure all bases were covered, the law excluded "persons who believe in or advocate the overthrow by force or violence of the Government of the United States or of all government or of all forms of law, or the assassination of public officials."

Anarchists already in the United States could be deported under the law. The first such case was that of John Turner, a trade union organizer and "philosophical anarchist" who had been in the United States since 1896. In spite of a protest meeting at Cooper Union and a defense by Clarence Darrow, the Supreme Court upheld Turner's deportation in 1903. According to a later commentator, "It was this deci-

sion of the Supreme Court which opened the way for the general policy of inquisition and exclusion so closely followed for a generation."

The manifest lists were later delivered to immigration authorities. Each manifest was designated with a letter of the alphabet, and the names were assigned numbers. Immigrants were given cards coded with their manifest sheets and numbers to present to examiners at Ellis Island. Thus the problem of identification was resolved in an era before drivers' licenses and social security numbers.

Most immigrants still traveled via steerage. While there was no doubt that conditions aboard steamships in the early 1900s had improved vastly over the sailing ships of sixty to eighty years earlier, substantial room for betterment remained. Kellogg Durand published an article in *The Independent* in 1906 detailing his experiences as a steerage passenger to Naples and back. While the price of first-class accommodations was two-and-a-half to three times the fare for steerage class ($75 to $90 for first class, $30 to $36 for steerage), Durand observed that "the difference in service . . . showed a discrepancy so startling that a conservative writer hesitates to estimate

Passing a cursory examination aboard the steamships, pilgrims to America were transported by barge from the New York docks to Ellis Island for full inspection and processing. (Photo courtesy of the Library of Congress)

The barges unloaded immigrants at a dock in front of the administration buildings on Ellis Island. The railings and protective wiring on the west wing rooftop (left) surround the "roof garden," where immigrants could exercise. (Photo courtesy of the New York Public Library)

it." After describing the overcrowding, poor treatment, lack of services, and substandard food apportioned to steerage passengers, Durand wrote: "If human beings are to be subjected to treatment and conditions proper for cattle, then they should be taken at freight or live stock rates; or, on the other hand, if they are to be called passengers and charged a substantial passenger rate, then they should have the consideration of such."

As the voyagers neared their final destination, joy was tempered with fears of rejection at the "Batteria," the expression writer Broughton Brandenburg heard a group of Italian immigrants use in reference to the entire examination process. To gather material for a series of magazine articles on immigration, Brandenburg and his wife accompanied a family of Italians in steerage from Naples in 1903. After passing the quarantine doctors at Sandy Hook, Brandenburg reported, passengers rushed to see the buildings of Manhattan as the ship sailed into the harbor. The immigrants also marveled at the Statue of Liberty— "that great beacon whose significance is so much to them, standing within the portals of the New World and proclaiming the liberty, justice, and equality they had never known, proclaiming a life in which they have an opportunity such as never could come to them elsewhere."

Once the ship docked, it was boarded by immigrant landing inspectors and a medical officer, who examined the cabin-class passengers. Most were passed through quickly, free to go through customs at the Barge Office, but usually a few were detained for the trip to Ellis Island. (A ruse that had been employed earlier, when cabin-class examinations were *pro forma*, was for a family to buy a second-class ticket for a family member who might not pass inspection at Ellis Island. This technique was not so effective after closer examinations of these passengers took place aboard the vessels early in the twentieth century.) Finally the steerage passengers were loaded onto barges destined for Ellis Island. If arrivals at the island were particularly heavy, the passengers would wait aboard the steamship, sometimes for days.

At the island the immigrants remained aboard barges until room opened for them to join the line streaming into the building. They first entered a baggage room, where they left their possessions, then proceeded up a long staircase leading from the baggage room to the second-floor registry room. Public Health Service doctors at the top of the stairs surreptitiously watched the immigrants climb the distance between floors. This was the "six-second medical examination," where doctors watched particularly for lameness or shortness of breath. Doctors throughout the building used a coded letter system to indicate problems for which further examinations were necessary. An *L* chalked on a person's right coat front or lapel meant a suspicion of lameness. *B* indicated back problems; *F*, face; *Ft*, feet; *E*, eyes; and so on.

After entering the registry room, the immigrants went through a two- to three-minute medical examination, with particular attention paid to the posture, walk, and eyes of the individual. If the examiner noted any signs of physical or mental defects, the ever-present chalk mark appeared on the coat and the subject was sent to an area of wire compartments to await further medical tests. If this examination revealed no serious problems, the immigrant rejoined the process. Some, however, were confined to a hospital on the island for further study or treatment. Others were deported immediately.

The legal examination followed the medical inspection. Here immigrants were queried about their age, dependency, financial status, and other issues on the original manifest lists, and, after 1917, submitted to a literacy test. Translators were required, and the immigration service was always on the lookout for enterprising young men who could converse in any of a dozen or so languages and dialects. Following the 1909 order of Commissioner Williams, the aliens were also required at this point to show that they were in possession of the equivalent of $25.

About 80 percent of the immigrants who landed at Ellis Island passed through all of these examinations without difficulties. Among the other 20 percent, some were retained for mental testing. In earlier times the mental tests consisted of simple conversa-

During the foreign influx as many as three thousand new residents of the United States were released daily. They faced one more line—the passenger queue for the ferryboat ride to their new home in America. (Photo courtesy of the Theodore Koch Collection, Michigan Historical Collections, Bentley Historical Library, the University of Michigan)

tions with the doctors. This sometimes led to confusion, as inspector Philip Cowan noted in his autobiography. He tested the intelligence of a heavyset son of Erin thus:

> "Pat, if I gave you two dogs and my friend here gave you one, how many would you have?" "Four, sir," says Pat. "Did you ever go to school, Pat?" "Yes indeed, sir." "Now, Pat, if you had an apple and I gave you one, how many would you have?" "Two, sir." "And if my friend gave you one, how many would you have?" "Three, sir." Then repeating the original question, the answer was again "Four, sir." "Why, Pat, how is that?" "Why, sure, I've got a dog at home meself."

Developed by Assistant Surgeon Howard A. Knox and adopted in 1913, "psychotesting" was designed to eliminate such ambiguities. Subjects were asked to select designs (of faces or leaves) that matched and to fit pegs into properly shaped holes in wooden frames. (Cowan claimed that one of the tests stumped a medical officer on the island.)

All who were rejected on medical, mental, or legal grounds could appeal to a three-member Board of Special Inquiry. The board held a preliminary hearing with the immigrant alone. Following this meeting the immigrant's friends, relatives, or legal counsel could meet with the board to testify on behalf of the immigrant. If two of the board members found for deportation, the alien could appeal to the commissioner general of immigration for special consideration.

Many immigrants were detained on the island during mealtime, sometimes for several meals. The fare proffered by the private concessionaires was always a matter of controversy. Commissioner Williams took an active interest in the quality of food provided and on several occasions asked his assistant commissioner to report the bill of fare to him. One such menu in 1906 consisted of:

BREAKFAST: coffee with milk and sugar, and bread and butter. Crackers and milk for women and children.

DINNER: Beef stew, boiled potatoes and rye bread. Smoked or pickled herring for Hebrews. Crackers and milk for women and children.

SUPPER: Baked beans, stewed prunes and rye bread, and tea with milk and sugar. Crackers and milk for women and children.

The biggest problem faced by the kitchen staff was the variety of diets favored by immigrants from all over the earth. Even the Europeans exhibited a

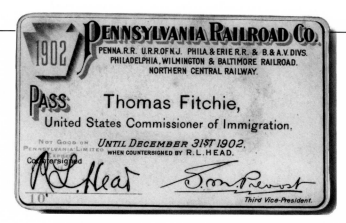

great diversity in tastes. To an Italian a meal without pasta was strange fare; others did not even know what pasta was. One woman who was given a plate of spaghetti with sauce thought she was being served "worms and blood."

In all, only about 2 percent of immigrants during this period failed to meet entrance requirements and were deported. The others were free to purchase ferry and railway tickets to their destinations and go about the business of becoming Americans. For most this meant changing out of their native costumes as soon as possible. An "amusing sight" of the time, according to later commissioner Edward Corsi, was the scene at the Battery when the Ellis Island ferryboat landed with its human freight:

> Many people have told me that half an hour after the boat came in, the dressing rooms in the adjacent ferry-houses, the bushes at the lower end of Battery Park, and even the gutters along the sidewalks presented the appearance of a junk shop. Queer headgear of women lay about, the familiar black-visored caps of the men and boys, waists and skirts or coats and trousers that undoubtedly went well in the outlying districts of Moscow but would not go far in Manhattan without causing comment and ridicule.

Those who got rid of their native garb did not leave the Battery naked, of course. They were supplied with American clothes by relatives and friends who may have been embarrassed by the prospect of being seen with "greenhorns" in New York City.

The peak immigration era ended with a literal bang—the shot that killed Archduke Francis Ferdinand in Sarajevo in 1914. As "the lamps went out all over Europe," prospective immigrants from that continent joined the army, were drafted, or stayed home. Immigration figures, which in 1914 nearly reached the 1907 level, dropped the following year to 326,700. The decline continued during and immediately after the war:

1916	298,826
1917	295,403
1918	110,618
1919	141,132

Furthermore, the few immigrants who did come to America originated mainly from places other than Europe and came to destinations other than Ellis Island. By 1919 only 26,731 entered New York Harbor, about 19 percent of the American total. A few years earlier, officials on Ellis Island would have examined that many immigrants in a week of heavy arrivals.

As war broke out in Europe, President Woodrow Wilson appointed a reformer to administer Ellis Island. Commissioner Frederic C. Howe was a former Cleveland lawyer associated with municipal reform and an expert on city planning. Active in politics, he had been an Ohio state senator, secretary of the National Progressive Republican League, and a leader in the campaign of candidate John Purroy Mitchel, who was elected mayor of New York in 1914. Concerning immigration policy, one of the commissioner's associates wrote that Howe "had the progressive idea that the Government should be the best friend of the immigrant, until he became a citizen; that he should come to it for guidance and protection."

Howe saw this as a particular necessity during wartime. The European conflict exacerbated normal problems in the detention and deportation of immigrants. Many could not be returned to their countries of origin under wartime conditions. The Department of Labor also prohibited deportations "to any ports where the return passage involved serious risks." Howe set out to humanize the Ellis Island facilities for the hundreds forced to live there for an extended time. He opened the lawns for outdoor recreation, initiated calisthenics classes, and equipped the island

◀ *Thinking to impress the inspectors, immigrants donned their "Sunday best" before arriving at Ellis Island. Consequently, visitors to the island were treated to a colorful display of native costumes like these worn by this Russian cossack (top left), this flute player (top right), these Dutch women (bottom left), and these Africans (bottom right). But when the immigrants left Ellis Island, many had changed into the American fashions brought by relatives and friends. (Photos courtesy of the National Park Service)*

Commissioner Frederic C. Howe thought that government (represented by Ellis Island) should be the immigrant's best friend. He humanized the immigration process by opening lawns for outdoor recreation, initiating calisthenics classes, and hanging swings for children. The "roof garden" on one wing of the administration building became a popular place for children to play and practice at waving Old Glory. (Photo courtesy of the National Park Service)

with swings for children and handball courts for men. He began a kindergarten for children and found employment (and entry to America) for more than three hundred adults who were to be deported on the grounds of immorality.

With Howe's encouragement a number of local organizations also came to the assistance of the detainees. Some donated materials for women's sewing classes. New York and New Jersey musical groups gave Sunday afternoon concerts on the island for over a year. Films were shown. Ethnic groups came to entertain and to visit. The New York Board of Education cooperated by arranging for the teaching of classes in English and other elementary subjects to the forty or fifty children on the island. Howe defined his own social thinking in an article he wrote for *The Survey* in 1916:

> Nothing has so confirmed my philosophy that the wrongs of the world, the evil, the vice, and the criminal actions of people are traceable back to the environment in which people live—to bad housing, to inadequate wages, to lack of decent recreation, as the way America absorbs and builds up discards whenever they are given a fair chance. All that seems to be necessary is a little help, a job and a minimum of attention. The experience of a year and a half at Ellis Island has convinced me that the evils usually ascribed to the badness of people are social in their origin. They are not traceable to the inherent viciousness of people. They are traceable to the inherent badness of our social order.

Howe attempted to use Ellis Island as a laboratory for social experimentation to prove his theories. Not all of his efforts, however, met with general approbation. Attempts to get more staffing and to raise wages for the efficient staff members fell on deaf ears in Washington. Remarking that the commissioner general did not even answer such requests, Howe claimed he "learned how we were governed by petty clerks, mostly Republicans. The government was their government." When he wanted to replace the private concessionaires on the island, Howe ran headlong into controversy. Congressman William S. Bennet of New York, formerly an attorney for the Ellis

Island food contractor, prevented Howe's action. He called Howe "a half-baked radical, who has free-love ideas" and criticized him for opening recreation areas where men, women, and children commingled. "This condition," Bennet declared, "if persisted in, will be far more harmful to the city of New York than the scourge of infantile paralysis."

While enabling Howe to make his humanizing

With Commissioner Howe's encouragement, the Salvation Army and other religious and ethnic groups often came to entertain and visit immigrants detained on the island. (Photo courtesy of the Theodore Koch Collection, Michigan Historical Collections, Bentley Historical Library, University of Michigan)

▲ *While much was made of the dining hall inadequacies, there were positive moments, such as this 1920 Passover seder for immigrants and the Ellis Island staff. Providing religious celebrations was a simple way to humanize the inspection process and begin assimilating Old World customs into New World lifestyles. (Photo courtesy of the YIVO Institute for Jewish Research)*

Processing successfully completed, immigrants often rushed to see the skyscraper cityscape of New York City. This father proudly points out the wonders of Manhattan to his wife, four daughters, and two sons. (Photo courtesy of the Theodore Koch Collection, Michigan Historical Collections, Bentley Historical Library, University of ▼ *Michigan)*

Some of Howe's suggested reforms were not as well received as the Sunday afternoon concerts for the immigrants conducted by New York and New Jersey musical groups. This "Americanization" concert was performed by the National Symphony Orchestra on September 19, 1921. (Photo courtesy of the Theodore Koch Collection, Michigan Historical Collections, Bentley Historical Library, University of Michigan)

changes, the conflict in Europe did not actually affect the immigration station until the early morning hours of July 30, 1916, when the war came directly to Ellis Island. That night German saboteurs set fire to explosives loaded on barges at the piers of the National Storage Company on the Black Tom River in nearby New Jersey. The barges were full of powder and shells to be towed downriver to a waiting Russian vessel, for use in the war. The initial huge explosion, followed by detonations for the next three hours, shattered windows on Manhattan from the Battery to 14th Street.

When the ammunition exploded, panic erupted on Ellis Island as windows blew out, doors jammed, and parts of roofs collapsed. The 353 immigrants sleeping in the main dormitory, along with 129 in the hospitals, were rushed outside in case of the need for emergency evacuation. Some of the "mentally disturbed" patients cheered at the fireworks display that lit up the night, as though it were a gigantic entertainment planned for their viewing pleasure.

Two fiery barges ran aground in the shallow water five hundred feet from the island, where they posed a greater threat to the immigration station than had the original explosion. They were finally towed out to sea and sunk by courageous sailors on two tugboats owned by the Lehigh Valley Railroad. Repairs to the island buildings ultimately cost $400,000, but miraculously, as in the case of the 1897 fire, no lives were lost and only minor injuries were reported. (Included in the injury report was an island cat cut by flying glass.)

When the United States entered the war in April 1917, German and Austrian ships, crews, and passengers in American harbors were seized. Along with the crews and passengers from these vessels, enemy nationals considered a threat to the United States, including suspected spies, were interned on Ellis Island for the duration of the war. This necessitated a change in use for some of the island's facilities, but Howe was determined to treat these prisoners of war like other detainees, with humanity and compassion. While a group of Germans complained about their treatment, Howe responded that "these complaints arise almost wholly from the fact that Ellis Island is not suited for long detentions; but the conditions now prevailing would probably be found any place and these enemy aliens far worse provided for if they were in open camp."

". . . the long journey is over, the new life begun. Those who have no friends run the gauntlet of the boarding-house runners and take their chances with the new freedom, unless the missionary or "the society" of their people holds out a helping hand. For at the barge-office gate Uncle Sam lets go. Through it they must walk alone."
—*Jacob Riis,* Century Magazine, *1903*

As the country geared up for war, other changes had to be made. Because of its location, portions of the island were sought for war-related uses by the army and the navy in 1918. Both services used the hospital facilities, as well as the baggage and dormitory building, the railroad ticket office, and parts of the main building. Consequently, sick immigrants and detainees were sent to hospitals in the New York area, long-term detainees were transferred to the Philadelphia immigration station, and enemy aliens were shipped to other detention camps.

By 1918 the immigration service was hardly functioning on Ellis Island. But the war would wind down by November, ending the presence of the army and the navy in island buildings, and immigrants would again begin to arrive at Ellis Island on the way to the land of hope and opportunity. However, the new arrivals would find the door to the United States open only a crack, as restrictionists had their way in the years just ahead.

THE ELLIS ISLAND EXPERIENCE

(circa 1907)

Developed over decades at both Castle Garden and Ellis Island, the inspection process was very efficient, almost mechanical at times. Although most immigrants spent an average of three hours on the island (even in 1907, the island's busiest year), the experience was a vivid memory for the rest of their lives.

While still aboard ship, the immigrants were given inspection cards and divided into groups of thirty. These groups were taken by barge to Ellis Island and would stay together throughout the inspection process.

The barges unloaded immigrants in front of the administration building, and the groups proceeded to the first-floor entrance. The entire east end of the first floor was devoted to baggage, and immigrants were encouraged to check their personal belongings for the duration of the inspection process. From the baggage check the group would climb a central stairway to the registry room (also called the Great Hall) on the second floor.

Immigrants were required to undergo two examinations: medical and legal. The central stairway helped to divide the second floor in half, with the east end set up for the medical examination and the west for the legal examination. The space was further divided by piping and wire into sections that accommodated thirty people. (Although done to maintain order, the structures reminded observers of the cattle pens in a stockyard.)

The medical exam started before the immigrants even reached the second floor. Medical inspectors were stationed at the top of the stairs to watch as the immigrants climbed. Any that showed difficulty with the climb had a letter code marked in chalk on his or her left lapel or coat front to alert other medical examiners.

At the top of the stairs, doctors spent about six minutes examining each immigrant for any physical or mental condition that might prevent the immigrant from earning a living, and also for symptoms of communicable or venereal disease. Any immigrant showing signs of such a condition was hospitalized or was detained for a more thorough examination (about twenty minutes) in one of the private examination rooms around the perimeter of the registry room.

Upon passing the medical exam, the immigrants proceeded through the maze of wire and piping toward the west end of the room where the legal exam was conducted. The legal exam consisted mainly of verifying the information on the ship's manifest, determining that each immigrant had enough money for a train ticket or a night's lodging, and, in later years, determining that each immigrant could read and write. If there was any discrepancy between the information provided and the answers given, the immigrant was detained to appear before a Board of Special Inquiry.

Successfully completing the legal exam, immigrants were issued a landing card and were free to enter the United States. A stairway at the west end of the registry room led back to the first floor, where a number of services were provided for immigrants. Workers at the Money Exchange would change foreign currency to U.S. dollars. Every railroad maintained a ticket office on Ellis Island. Many religious and charitable organizations kept offices on the island to assist immigrants. There was even a Post Office and a Western Union office at the west end of the first floor.

Miscellaneous business taken care of, immigrants collected their baggage and, with landing card prominently displayed, headed for the ferry or the railroad dock—the next leg on the journey to their new life.

In 1907, groups of new arrivals entered the main building, where they could check bulkier baggage before climbing the central staircase to the registry room on the second floor and examinations by medical and legal inspectors. Most immigrants passed these examinations and returned to the first floor on their way to their new life and homeland. (Illustration by Rosemary Morrissey-Herzberg)

New arrivals, like these Jewish immigrants, were gathered into groups of thirty (the capacity of the barge) and tagged with coded inspection cards. Their next stop would be Ellis Island. (Photo courtesy of Brown Brothers)

The queues began under the dockside awning, prior to actually entering the main building. (Photo courtesy of the New York Public Library)

At the height of immigration, the entire first floor of the administration building was converted into a makeshift baggage storage and claim area. But there was no centralized system, so some immigrants, like this Italian family of 1905, lost their baggage. (Photo by Lewis W. Hine, courtesy of the New York Public Library)

Before beginning the inspection process, immigrants were encouraged to check their personal belongings; however, the heavy influx of immigrants often found the baggage room filled beyond capacity. (Photo courtesy of the Theodore Koch Collection, Michigan Historical Collections, Bentley Historical Library, University of Michigan)

Doctors surreptitiously watched each person climb the stairs from the baggage area. If they spotted anything awry, like lameness or shortness of breath, a coded letter for the potential problem was chalked on the immigrant's lapel; the chalk-marked recipient might be sent to a detention cell to await a more thorough medical examination. (Photo courtesy of Brown Brothers)

The standard medical exam, which took just two to three minutes, included an eye exam, in which the upper eyelids were folded back over a special instrument that resembled a buttonhook. The most common reason for failing this test was trachoma, a contagious and chronic eye disease. (Photo courtesy of the National Park Service)

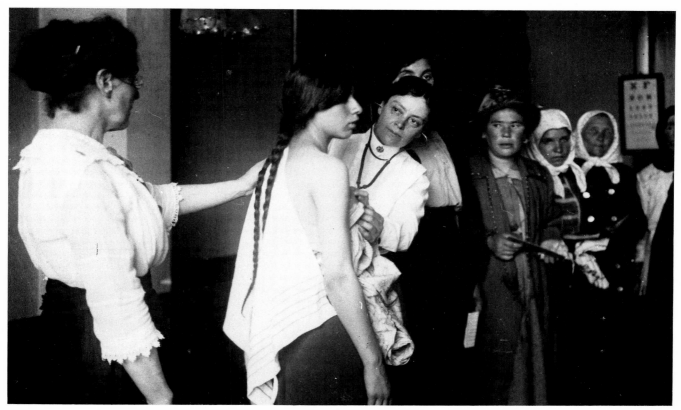

If the immigrant passed each of these quick medical tests, he or she could proceed to the main part of registry room. If the problem seemed minor but required closer scrutiny, immigrants were directed to one of the examining rooms around the perimeter of the Great Hall. Here nurses conduct a physical examination of these women. (Photo courtesy of the U.S. Department of Health)

Still in groups of thirty, immigrants moved from section to section in the "cattle pen," awaiting their turn for the legal exam. These mazes of piping and wire helped immigration inspectors make some order out of bedlam. (Photo courtesy of the New York Public Library)

The full immigration process took between three and five hours. But during the height of the foreign influx newcomers could be detained a full day or more. The immigration service offered free meals (subsidized by the steamship companies) to immigrants on the island during mealtime. This dining room in the kitchen, restaurant, and bath house building seated twelve hundred people. (Photo courtesy of the New York Public Library)

When their turn came, entrants lined up in front of the legal exam desk. Immigration officials used the legal exam to detain prostitutes, contract laborers, people apparently suffering from mental illness, and those who were destitute for further examination or questioning. (Photo courtesy of the Theodore Koch Collection, Michigan Historical Collections, Bentley Historical Library, University of Michigan)

This is the view from behind the legal inspector's desk. Inspectors handled four to five hundred immigrants from several continents daily. During the legal inspection immigrants were allowed interpreters. Most of the questions merely confirmed information that was on the manifest. (Photo courtesy of the Theodore Koch Collection, Michigan Historical Collections, Bentley Historical Library, University of Michigan)

Each immigrant spent about two minutes answering approximately thirty questions on subjects ranging from current financial status to final destination in the United States. In later years, immigrants also had to show that they had money, usually $25 in cash. About 80 percent of all applicants passed, receiving landing cards to enter the United States. (Photo courtesy of Brown Brothers)

Any immigrants who showed signs of mental deficiency during the legal exam were detained to undergo psychological testing. In earlier times the psychological testing often consisted of conversation between the examiner and the immigrant. After 1913 the psychological tests required prospective immigrants, like the woman above, to select matching designs of faces and leaves (see inset) or to fit pegs into properly shaped holes in wooden frames. The tests were developed by Assistant Surgeon Howard A. Knox. With the new tests, insanity certifications rose from 4.8 per hundred thousand in 1902 to 12.8 in 1913. Mental defects certification increased tenfold, from 5.1 per hundred thousand in 1902 to 50.8 in 1913. (Photo courtesy of Brown Brothers. Inset figure courtesy of the New York Public Library)

Having successfully completed the inspection process, immigrants were free to tie up the loose ends in their travel plans. They could exchange their native currency for American dollars at the Money Exchange. At the postal counter, they could send telegrams and postcards to family and friends. (Photo courtesy of the State Historical Society of Wisconsin)

The railroad ticket agents on Ellis Island always did a brisk business since only one-third of the immigrants remained in New York City. On a busy day they might sell as many as twenty-five tickets a minute to the new Americans. (Photo courtesy of the State Historical Society of Wisconsin)

Their landing cards prominently and proudly displayed, these newest Americans board the ferry that will carry them to their new homeland. (Photo courtesy of the State Historical Society of Wisconsin)

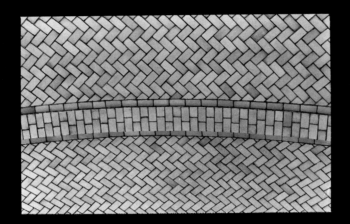

Six

The Decline of Ellis Island, 1917–1954

Each successive era brought changes to Ellis Island. The war years had wrought additional physical changes. The structures damaged by the Black Tom explosions included the main building, where the ceiling was destroyed beyond repair. To replace it, island officials hired the Guastavino Brothers, Italian immigrant masons famous for their tile work. (They installed the ceiling for what became the Oyster Bar in Grand Central terminal.) They used a process of interlocking dovetailed tiling to form the huge vaulted ceiling in the Great Hall, or registry room. Working without scaffolding, the masons applied mortar and tiles while hanging from safety belts attached to the roof.

The other major project was rebuilding the seawall along the ferry slip between Islands Number 1 and Number 2. Starting just outside the cribwork walls, the builders dredged a trench in which they hardened bags of concrete in the water as a foundation. Railroad rails were placed on top of the concrete to make a level bed and were cemented into place. Divers smoothed the concrete atop the rails. After this foundation was set, huge concrete blocks seventeen feet high and twelve feet wide, weighing eighty-seven tons apiece, were lowered into the water on top of concrete. Finally a concrete, granite-faced wall was built on top of the blocks.

New construction and repairs were by no means the most important changes on the island following the war. In the decades to come, Ellis Island would decline in importance as an inspection station, as immigration slowed to a trickle. A renewed reaction against aliens—all aliens—set in following the war.

◀ *Interlocking dovetailed tiles clad the Great Hall's vaulted ceiling. The Guastavino Brothers, Italian-American masons renowned for their masterworks, installed the tiling without the benefit of scaffolding. Instead they dangled from safety belts attached to the roof. (Photo courtesy of Wilton S. Tifft)*

It seemed almost as though the citizenry pondered the question during the lull from 1917 to 1919, built up a suspicion and hatred of foreigners as a result of the war and the Russian Revolution, and collectively decided to restrict immigration at the war's end. Ellis Island would never be the same.

The movement to restrict immigration actually had been gaining momentum for some time. Commissioners Watchorn and Williams, echoing many book and magazine writers, had suggested tighter immigration laws for years. The Dillingham Commission, appointed by President Theodore Roosevelt, spent nearly four years studying the matter and issued a forty-two-volume report in 1911. Few, if any, people waded through the mass of testimony and statistics, but the report's recommendations were discussed widely. These recommendations called for stricter immigration laws, based on a number of "principles" that guided the commission. The most significant were these two:

1. While the American people, as in the past, welcome the oppressed of other lands, care should be taken that immigration be such both in quality and quantity as not to make too difficult the process of assimilation.
4. The development of business may be brought about by means which lower the standard of living of the wage earners. A slow expansion of industry which would permit the adaptation and assimilation of the incoming labor supply is preferable to a very rapid industrial expansion which results in the immigration of laborers of low standards and efficiency, who imperil the American standard of wages and conditions of employment.

The successful arguments for restriction in the 1800s and early 1900s were based on the assumption that certain classes of people were mentally or phys-

Refugees of war often sought asylum in the United States, and sometimes the queuing began an ocean away from Ellis Island. These refugees are waiting outside the American consulate in Warsaw, Poland. (Photo courtesy of the YIVO Institute for Jewish Research)

American attitudes toward immigration changed after WWI and restrictionist arguments were heard by more sympathetic ears. The Hebrew Sheltering Society, which paid for these immigrants' transportation, assured American restrictionists that the women on board were homemakers and would not be thrust into manufacturing jobs. (Photo courtesy of the Theodore Koch Collection, Michigan Historical Collections, Bentley Historical Library, University of Michigan)

Eastern Europeans leave Ellis Island after acceptance. Many of these immigrants will find jobs along the northeastern seaboard, in the corridor running from New York City to Washington, D.C. Others will head inland to Chicago and points farther west. After 1917, all of them had to prove they could read and write. (Photo courtesy of UPI/Bettmann Newsphotos)

ically unfit to earn a living and contribute to American life. Around the time of World War I, however, the emphasis of the restrictionists changed. Always fearful of the collapse of the American Dream under the onslaught of the new immigrant peasants from southern and eastern Europe, the nativists began to push more aggressively for a new program to broaden restriction. Instrumental to the acceptance of this idea were writers who developed "racial" theories to explain why America must bar the immigrants. Foremost among them was a New York anthropologist and anti-Semite, Madison Grant.

Grant stated frankly that some of the European races were inferior to others. He utilized a crude interpretation of Mendelian genetics to "prove" that the intermingling of the superior and inferior races would degrade the former. The title of his 1916 book, *The Passing of the Great Race*, reflected his prediction for America's future given unrestricted immigration. He wrote of the "racial nondescripts who are now flocking here":

> These new immigrants were no longer exclusively members of the Nordic race as were the earlier ones who came of their own impulse to improve their social conditions. The transportation lines advertised America as a land flowing with milk and honey and the European governments took the opportunity to unload upon care-

less, wealthy and hospitable America the sweepings of their jails and asylums. . . . The new immigration . . . contained a large and increasing number of the weak, the broken and the mentally crippled of all races drawn from the lowest stratum of the Mediterranean basin and the Balkans, together with hordes of the wretched, submerged population of the Polish ghettos. Our jails, insane asylums, and alms-houses are filled with this human flotsam. . . .

> These immigrants adopt the language of the native American, they wear his clothes, they steal his name and they are beginning to take his women, but they seldom adopt his religion or understand his ideals, and while he is being elbowed out of his own home the American looks calmly abroad and urges on others the suicidal ethics which are exterminating his own race.

Grant's book was a bestseller. The philosophy behind it prompted the passage (over President Wilson's veto) of the new, comprehensive Immigration Law of 1917. The new law contained thirty-three categories of aliens to be excluded, including those over sixteen who could not read some language. (An exception was granted to close relatives of aliens already legally admitted to the United States.) Deportation rules were also changed. Prior to 1917 an alien could be deported for cause within three years of

Most new arrivals flocked to areas already settled by countrymen who had immigrated earlier. In the cities this gave rise to the ethnic neighborhoods, like the Jewish quarter on New York City's East Side pictured here. In the heartland and the west, whole communities took on an ethnic flavor. But although these groupings helped assimilate the new immigrants, they also fueled suspicion and fear. (Photo by Lewis W. Hine, courtesy of the New York Public Library)

These Italian men were hoping for a warm reception by their adopted country. Unfortunately, American attitudes changed after WWI, and instead, newcomers in the 1920s were met with quotas. (Photo courtesy of the International Museum of Photography at George Eastman House)

entry; this was now extended to five years. Furthermore, anarchists, aliens associated with prostitution, and former felons could be deported at any time. On the administrative side, the law provided for increased inspection of prospective immigrants at foreign ports and aboard ships before they reached the United States, a change urged by immigration officials.

Legislation passed in 1918 broadened the definition of the deportable class to include not only those holding anarchistic beliefs or advocating the overthrow of the United States government but also members of proscribed organizations and aliens writing, publishing, or even possessing publications about anarchism. Passed as a response to the Russian Revolution and subsequent developments in Europe, the law would be applied against radicals in America in actions one government official later called the "Deportations Delirium of 1920."

◀ *In New York City's East Side tenements, running water might be a community spigot in the hallway. Americans might consider these poor living conditions, but they were an improvement for most immigrants. Besides, unlike the Old World, with hard work there was hope of improving one's standard of living. (Photo by Lewis W. Hine, courtesy of the New York Public Library)*

In the 1920s the origins of immigrants remained diverse, but their numbers dropped dramatically under the new, strict quotas legislated in 1924. (Photo courtesy of the National Parks Service: Statue of Liberty National Monument)

The Russian Revolution of 1917 posed the threat of international communism to the rest of the world. This in itself was a frightening specter to the United States, where radical labor activity in the late nineteenth century had met with violence. When Russia withdrew from WWI and concluded a separate peace treaty with Germany in 1918, antiradical sentiments were further inflamed. Many American socialists had refused to support the American war effort in 1917 and 1918 and were charged with trying to subvert the "100-percent Americanism" the war crisis demanded. The stage was set for an antiradical outburst in the United States.

It came in 1919. Beginning early in the year with a general strike in Seattle, which the mayor there claimed (to his own political advantage) was fomented by the forces of international communism, a reaction against all forms of radicalism spread across the country and produced the "Red Scare" of 1919–1920. Suspected radicals were arrested in massive raids in 1919, and aliens among them were ordered summarily deported by the Justice Department, headed by the virulently antiradical attorney general, A. Mitchell Palmer. The deportees went to Ellis Island.

The first group of detained aliens, mostly members of the Industrial Workers of the World, active in promoting labor organization in western lumber camps, came in February 1919. Others followed in March and through the summer months. Commissioner Howe, upon his return from the peace conference at Versailles, protested the deportation without hearings of hundreds of aliens. His campaign to uphold the civil rights of the alleged radicals failed. Resigning "in a state of bitterness" in September 1919, he later wrote, "I had entered whole-heartedly into my principality of Ellis Island, hoping to make it a playhouse for immigrants. I left a prison."

After Howe resigned, the Justice Department initiated a new series of raids. More than six hundred aliens were sent to Ellis Island to await deportation. The most famous among them was Emma Goldman, a Russian-born anarchist who had entered the United States through Castle Garden in 1885. She was one of 249 aliens who were held late in 1919 for eventual deportation to Russia. They were shipped just before Christmas aboard the *Buford*, which the press dubbed the "Soviet Ark." She later described the conditions prevailing on the island for incoming aliens who were detained:

The condition of the emigrants on Ellis Island was nothing short of frightful. Their quarters were congested, the food was abominable, and they were treated like felons. These unfortunates had cut their moorings in the homeland and had pilgrimed to the United States as the land of promise, liberty, and opportunity. Instead they

With housing conditions in the New World almost as poor as those in the Old World, some newcomers found that immigrating meant changing address but not standard of living. (Photo courtesy of the Museum of the City of New York)

Manufacturing businesses benefited from the flood tide of immigrants. Cheap labor was ample for even the basest of tasks. In the early twentieth century, mass-production factories were coming into their own, thanks to immigrant working women, like these workers shaping cigars. But restriction of cheap immigrant labor through quotas and enactment of the labor laws would put an end to the sweatshops. (Photo courtesy of the International Museum of Photography at George Eastman House)

To make financial ends meet the whole immigrant family often pitched in. This mother and her children are doing feather piecework at home. It was this willingness to work long hours for low wages that worried established labor and fueled the restrictionist rhetoric. (Photo courtesy of the Library of Congress)

Like these coalbreakers in a Pennsylvania shaft, immigrants often were willing to work under tough occupational conditions for low hourly wages. The new child labor laws would make this a rare scene in the 1920s. (Photo courtesy of the International Museum of Photography at George Eastman House)

The railways also had work for America's new residents. This Italian trackwalker for the Pennsylvania Railroad trekked the tracks, tightening or replacing loose and damaged linkages between the wooden ties and the metal rails. (Photo by Lewis W. Hine, courtesy of the New York Public Library)

Many eastern Europeans found jobs in Pennsylvania's coal country. This Slavic miner worked in the Pittsburgh District. The cap won't protect him from falling rocks, but it is equipped for oil-fueled lighting. (Photo by Lewis W. Hine, courtesy of the New York Public Library)

Enthused by bestselling author Madison Grant, restrictionists sought to limit immigrants from southern and eastern Europe, like this young Italian girl. (Photo by Lewis W. Hine, courtesy of the New York Public Library)

found themselves locked up, ill-treated, and kept in uncertainty for months.

The deportations and the Red Scare ended. The nativism and xenophobia did not. As historian William Leuchtenberg pointed out, most Americans at the end of the war were disposed to agree with the statement of Walter Hines Page, former United States ambassador to England: "We Americans have got to . . . hang our Irish agitators and shoot our hyphenates and bring up our children with reverence for English history and in the awe of English literature."

Immigration numbers in 1920 picked up where they had left off before the war. The figures for 1921 doubled those of 1920. From mid-1920 to mid-1921, more than eight hundred thousand immigrants sought admission. The floodgates of Europe were open again. Ellis Island, with its staff still low from the war years, could not handle the flow. Ships backed up in the harbor and were diverted to Boston and other ports. A contemporary cartoon showed swarms of alien peasants flying over the ocean and landing on a rocky promontory. Nearby stood a dismayed-looking congressman holding a blunderbuss labeled "Immigration Laws," while a man informed him, "You can't stop 'em with that old gun, Congress."

Congress found its new "gun" in the form of the first "quota" law, based on the concept of "national origins," passed in 1921. The temporary emergency

The Nordic "race" was more well received during the restrictionist era. Author Grant and his followers thought that Mediterranean Basin immigrants were dumped on America's shores, while the Scandinavians "came of their own impulse to improve their social conditions." (Photo courtesy of the National Park Service)

act was signed by President Warren G. Harding in May after Wilson had pocket-vetoed it three months earlier. The quota system in the bill restricted immigration from any given country in a single year to 3 percent of the people from that nation already living in the United States as reported in the census of 1910. Historian John Higham described the effects of the law:

Ellis Island often is considered the open door through which immigrants gained access to new horizons. But it also was the door that locked behind deported labor activists, such as Alexander Berkman (left) and anarchist Emma Goldman (right). This photo was taken shortly before Berkman was banished to Russia along with 248 other alleged radicals on the SS Buford a few days before Christmas in 1919. Goldman had entered through Castle Garden in 1885 and left through Ellis Island in 1919 also on the SS Buford. (Berkman photo courtesy of the George G. Bain Collection, Library of Congress; Goldman photo courtesy of the National Park Service)

Although adopted as very temporary legislation, the law of 1921 proved in the long run the most important turning point in American immigration policy. It imposed the first sharp and absolute numerical limits on European immigration. It established a national quota system based on the preexisting composition of the American population—an idea which has survived in one form or another through all subsequent legislation. It ensured especially that the new immigration could not reach more than a small fraction of its prewar level. Above all, the policy now adopted meant that in a generation the foreign-born would cease to be a major factor in American history.

The law went into effect in June 1921 for a year. It was renewed annually thereafter until the passage of a permanent quota law in 1924. The total number of immigrants to be allowed into the country during fiscal year 1922 was 355,825. The quota limits, for all countries with a quota over one thousand, were:

United Kingdom	77,342	Yugoslavia	6,426
Germany	68,059	France	5,729
Italy	42,057	Denmark	5,694
Russia	34,284	Hungary	5,638
Poland (including		Finland	3,921
Eastern Galicia)	25,827	Switzerland	3,752
Sweden	20,042	Netherlands	3,607
Czechoslovakia	14,282	Greece	3,294
Norway	12,202	Portugal	2,520
Austria	7,451	Armenia	1,589
Romania	7,419	Belgium	1,563

These figures alone indicate the intent of the law. The northern and western European nations in this group were permitted 209,362 immigrants, the southern and eastern nations 143,336. While this disparity does not seem extraordinary, the fact was that the ratio of new immigrants to old had been nearly four to one in the years just prior to the war. The lawmakers clearly sought to exclude the great masses of new immigrants. While 95.3 percent of the quotas for southern and eastern European countries were

Deportation conditions in 1919–1920 were deplorable. Quarters for deportees were the same steerage-class accommodations some of them had suffered through to come to America a couple of decades earlier. This photo by Alfred Stieglitz illustrates the overcrowding typical of steerage. (Photo courtesy of the Library of Congress)

Immigration quotas were first legislated in 1921. The law was based on the national census of 1910 and favored the northern and western segments of Europe. The result was a Caucasian immigrant as the norm, with far fewer places at America's table for Asians or Africans. (Photo courtesy of UPI/Bettmann Newsphotos)

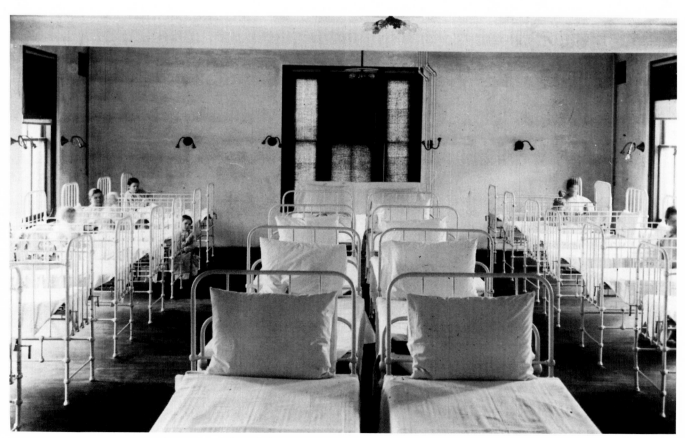

Fewer immigrants meant less usage of Ellis Island's specialized units. For example, the children's hospital ward (shown above), where youngsters were placed for observation and further medical testing, is only half full. During the flood tide years there was a serious bed shortage in this ward. (Photo courtesy of the National Park Service)

In Europe educational opportunity was often determined by social class. Consequently many immigrants were drawn to America's policy of universal public education as a way for the next generation to improve its lot in life. This is a classroom for the children of immigrants detained on Ellis Island. (Photo courtesy of the National Archives)

filled in 1921–1922, the countries forming the older American stock filled only 46.4 percent of their quotas in the first year. Supporters of restriction pointed to these figures as proof that the old immigration was exhausted and that Congress had acted just in time to close the door against supposedly less desirable aliens.

Such sentiments did not wane but became stronger as the 1920s passed. Sensationalist tabloid newspapers helped create the stereotype of the Italian-American as a gangster involved in the illegal liquor trade and in shoot-outs on big-city streets at least once a week. The Ku Klux Klan, which had been revived in 1915, experienced a surge of growth during the 1920s, fomenting not only racial prejudice against blacks and religious prejudice against Catholics but also hatred of immigrants. In the Sacco-Vanzetti case, which became the great liberal cause of the decade, it was obvious that the defendants, Nicola Sacco and Bartolomeo Vanzetti, did not receive a fair trial. They were subsequently executed, not on the basis of innocence or guilt, but because they were Italian immigrants with anarchist leanings. The decade of the 1920s was filled with examples of political and social fundamentalism, which augured ill for outsiders.

The Immigration Act of May 1924 continued the restriction of immigration on the basis of a quota system, but the quota was lowered to 2 percent, and the standard used for national origins was the census of 1890. This ensured that preference was accorded to immigrants from England and northern Europe, since the great flood of immigrants from Italy and eastern Europe had not come until after 1890. Of the 164,677 immigrants to be allowed under the new law, 85.6 percent were from the countries of northern and western Europe, with only 12.4 percent from the southern and eastern regions of the continent.

Another major change in immigration policy under the new law related to inspection. Immigrants were now required to demonstrate their admissibility to the United States before sailing, since they were required to obtain an immigration visa from a United States consular official abroad to qualify for admission on arrival. The American consulates closely observed the quota numbers for each month and year in issuing these visas.

Besides providing for inspection by officials in ports of origin, this new procedure ended a dangerous practice that had followed the passage of the original quota law in 1921. The quota year ran from July 1 to June 30. For countries with quotas smaller than prospective immigration, there was a great race to land ships on July 1, the beginning of the new quota year. Thereafter, it was imperative for an immigrant to be on a ship arriving early in the month since no more than 20 percent of the quota (10 percent under the 1924 law) could be admitted in any one

TWELVE SHIPS MAKE A MIDNIGHT DASH WITH 10,000 ALIENS

Presidente Wilson, Italian, First In; Canada, French, Second; Polonia, Dane, Third.

RACE TO BEAT JULY QUOTA

Commissioner Curran Will Be Assisted in Handling Crush by Washington Officials.

MANY WILL BE DEPORTED

One Vessel Is Bringing More Greeks Than the Law Will Allow to Enter.

Twelve steamships filled with immigrants eager to land in the United States are due to arrive in this port today and about 10,000 aliens hope that they will be in time for the July quota. To lessen the congestion at New York, the White Star liner Adriatic, the United

For countries with small immigration quotas, Ellis Island became the finish line in a great race across the ocean. The goal was to arrive in New York Harbor on July 1, when the new quota period began. It was a challenge well met, as this article excerpted from the July 1, 1923, edition of the New York Times *observes. (Newspaper reproduction courtesy of the* New York Times)

These two black children, waiting in the railroad ticket office for transporation to the train, came through a less crowded Ellis Island. If they had had to stay on the island, they would have found conditions more pleasant because of the efforts of Commissioners Frederic C. Howe, Henry Curran, and Edward Corsi. (Photo courtesy of the Library of Congress)

month. Henry Curran, commissioner at Ellis Island in 1923, wrote of this situation:

> Competing steamship companies would bring in immigrants from all over the world, trusting to win the race at the finish. It was dangerous to human life to have twenty great ships crowding through the Narrows at the stroke of midnight. It was tragedy to the immigrants who had pulled up stakes, left home behind, and come hopefully here only to be turned back at the gate, through no fault of their own, as "excess quota." They had no place to go—the old home gone, the new home forbidden—it was tragedy that tore the heartstrings of those of us who understood.

While all of these changes in the immigration laws came about, Ellis Island was administered by commissioners who followed Howe in spirit by attempting to make the island as pleasant as possible for persons detained there. Commissioner Curran, for example, found the dormitory facilities particularly inhospitable. "I never saw a jail as bad," he wrote. He secured new beds, additional recreation space, and several other improvements to the island. His success in obtaining appropriations from Washington for improvements was due in part to the fact that Ellis Island had become a subject for diplomacy between England and the United States in the early 1920s, which culminated in an inspection visit to the island

Commissioner Henry Curran improved Ellis Island's recreational facilties. Detainees enjoy the playing field while waiting for acceptance. (Photo courtesy of AP/World Wide Photos)

MONSTER MASS=MEETING

— TO PROTEST AGAINST —
 RESTRICTIONS OF IMMIGRATION

The demands of the restrictionists in Congress for the adoption of a literacy test, having for its purpose the exclusion from this country annually of thousands of Hebrews, Italians, and the representatives of other races, seeking opportunity and freedom under our flag, have despite the stinging defeat received by them through the efforts of Honorable JAMES M. CURLEY, and other able and equally courageous members of Congress, again brought the matter up for immediate consideration.

Upon **Thursday and Friday** of this week hearings will be held under the direction of Congressman JOHN L. BURNETT, the arch enemy of all foreigners, in an endeavor to secure immediate enactment into law of this harsh and oppressive measure.

CONGRESSMAN CURLEY

With a view to voicing a protest so loud that its echoes
will resound in the halls of Congress, will appear at the

MONSTER PROTEST MEETING

— TO BE HELD AT —

SCENIC TEMPLE, Blue Hill and Lawrence Avenues
on SUNDAY, DECEMBER 14, at 3.00 P. M.

AND AN EQUALLY MONSTER GATHERING IN THE CRADLE OF LIBERTY

FANEUIL HALL
SUNDAY, DEC. 14, at 8.00 p. m.

— HE HAS INVITED AND ACCEPTANCES HAVE BEEN RECEIVED FROM —

JUDGE LEON SANDERS
MANUEL F. BEHAR, all of New York
LOUIS LEVY, of Philadelphia
Hon. ANTONIO ZUCCA, of New York
Hon. JOHN J. FRECHI, of New York
Dr. S. J. DRABINSKY, of Brooklyn

Dr. HARRY LEVY, of Commonwealth Temple
Dr. RUBINOVITZ, Moreland St. Synagogue
Rabbi A. GOROVITZ, of Roxbury
Rabbi P. ISRAELI, Adath Jeshurun Synagogue
JACOB DE HAAS, Boston Jewish Advocate
EZEKIEL LEAVITT, Editor of Boston Voice

and others, and has received assurances from the foremost representatives of all races in Massachusetts, that they will attend

The duty we owe to those of our race and blood, the obligation we hold to our American citizenship, demands the presence of all at these meetings. Seats have been reserved for the ladies, and we should endeavor to make these two gatherings the most representative protest ever recorded in the history of Boston.

Boston Citizens League.

◀ *Not everyone sat idly by while the restrictionists campaigned openly. In the American tradition Bostonians were called to a Faneuil Hall rally ". . . with a view to voicing a protest so loud that its echoes will resound in the halls of Congress. . . ." (Poster courtesy of the National Park Service)*

in 1922 by the British ambassador. The topic of dissension was the treatment of British subjects at Ellis Island.

The British had always been troublesome at the immigration station. Commissioner Howe described the problem:

> When a British subject was detained, he rushed to the telephone to communicate with the consul-general in New York or the ambassador at Washington, protesting against the outrage. When ordered deported, he sizzled in his wrath over the indignities he was subjected to. All this was in effect a resentment that any nation should have the arrogance to interfere with a British subject in his movements. All Englishmen seemed to assume that they had a right to go anywhere they liked, and that any interference with this right was an affront to the whole British Empire.

Commissioner Edward Corsi later echoed these same sentiments. "It has always seemed to me that British

The Great Hall (registry room) in 1931 bore very little resemblance to its prisonlike "cattle pens" of the flood tide era. The raging immigration river reduced to a calm rivulet, the pipe-and-wire enclosures of the earlier era were gone, but the benches remained. The Ellis Island staff dwindled, building sections were closed, and many of the hospital facilities were used to treat alien seamen. (Photo courtesy of UPI/Bettmann Newsphotos)

The American Tract Society maintained Ellis Island's Welfare Library for both temporarily detained immigrants and deportees. Both recreational and educational reading materials were provided. (Photo courtesy of the Library of Congress)

By 1929 the immigrants passing through primary inspection at Ellis Island were from countries without consular ▶
inspection facilities. These French West Indies women who arrived on the SS Korona in 1911 would still have stopped at
Ellis Island if their boat had arrived in 1931. (Photo courtesy of the National Park Service)

criticism of the American immigration system was the cry of the aristocrat coming in close contact with those less cultured and dainty in their tastes and habits," he wrote.

Though some immigrants were disgusted by their treatment at Ellis Island, others found the experience joyous and inspiring. One was George Mardikian, a Greek who recalled his 1922 steerage voyage in his autobiography thirty-four years later. His fondest memory of Ellis Island was the shower, with all the hot water he wanted, in the dormitory building immediately after arrival:

> I began to sing. I stopped singing to splash and laugh, and then sang some more. The song and the beautiful, plentiful hot water were washing away the sweat and dust and grime of the steerage. I scrubbed harder and harder. I washed away the grime, and I washed away the years. I washed away the Old World. I washed away all the hatred and injustice and cruelty I had known, all the hunger, all the weeping, all the pain.

To Mardikian this shower was a kind of rebirth, a symbolic experience so powerful that he celebrated the date of it, July 24, as his birthday thereafter.

Whether immigrants found it inspiring or horrible, Ellis Island after the quota laws took effect was not what it had been. The commissioner general of immigration referred to this in his annual report for 1927. "If the expressions 'Ellis Island' and 'Immigration' were not synonymous," he wrote, "one could hardly think of the one without thinking of the other. Ellis Island was the great outpost of the new and vigorous Republic." By 1927, however, "Ellis Island is freed of this inundating horde and largely freed of carping critics, but Ellis Island has lost its proud place in the grand immigration scheme." The staff dwindled in number, sections of buildings were closed, and the Public Health Service commandeered three-quarters of the hospital facilities for the treatment of alien seamen. By 1929 the only immigrants to pass through primary inspection on the island were those from nonquota countries in the Western Hemisphere or from countries without consular inspection facilities. The new quota provisions that took effect on July 1, 1929, further reduced the number of immigrants to an annual limit of 150,000.

Events later in the year even more decisively decreased the total.

The Great Depression of the 1930s stifled immigration far more effectively than the efforts of lawmakers. Not until the end of World War II would a hundred thousand immigrants again pass through American ports in a single year. Many aliens already in America left. Not finding the economic opportunities they had hoped for, they returned to their homelands. (Some tried to save the price of passage home by being deported, "converting" to anarchism or manufacturing evidence to demonstrate that they were among the undesirable classes.) In 1932 the number of aliens that left the country was greater than the number that came in. This preponderance of out-migration continued until the end of the decade.

Departure of these aliens was not viewed as cause for alarm. With millions of Americans already unemployed, President Herbert Hoover did not need additional jobseekers. The Hoover administration, in fact, took steps to counter the unemployment problem by collecting and deporting all aliens who were in the country illegally. In the first few months under this policy more than a thousand radical, vagrant, or visaless aliens were deported, and hundreds more were detained on Ellis Island.

While the deportation program continued, Hoover selected as the new commissioner of Ellis Island Edward Corsi, a settlement-house director, who was told to "clean up the mess down there." The mess Corsi found at the island was the result of poor administration, low morale among the staff, and recent charges of racketeering on the part of Ellis Island employees.

Corsi realized that Ellis Island had a new role in the deportation business. He later wrote:

> I foresaw that a large portion of my duties would relate to deportation—that is, the weeding out of ugly and sick elements in our national life, and consequently, the vitalizing of that life in general. I should be a sort of physician to the whole country, delegated to cut out the cancers and amputate the infected limbs. I saw that this was not a new and isolated aspect of what is called the "immigration problem," but merely a result

Eventually even the benches in the Great Hall (registry room) disappeared. Settees and rocking chairs easily sat the few thousand immigrants entering Ellis Island during the 1930s. (Photo courtesy of the National Archives)

of the free and rapid growth of our country, which, if we look at it in the light of true history, had sprung up like a toadstool overnight.

This did not mean that Corsi entirely favored the wholesale deportation of aliens. "Our deportation laws are inexorable and in many cases inhuman," he observed, "particularly as they apply to men and women of honest behavior whose only crime is that they dared enter the promised land without conforming to law."

Like Commissioner Howe before him, Corsi set out to humanize conditions on the island in the belief that persons detained for deportation should not be treated as prisoners. Some of the changes he instituted included allowing friends and relatives to visit detainees every day, rather than twice a week as in the past, and allowing detainees to use telephones, to leave the island under guard, to communicate directly with Corsi, and to spend more time outdoors walking or engaging in recreational activities. He

obtained money from the Hoover administration to build a new records room and to demolish the old canopy at the front of the main building, which he replaced with a pleasant plaza of flower beds.

When Franklin D. Roosevelt took office in March 1933, he extended Corsi's appointment. Although he resigned in January 1934 in order to serve as director of relief programs in New York City under Mayor Fiorello La Guardia, Corsi left as a legacy many recommendations that the Roosevelt administration followed. The New Dealers spent more than $1 million on these projects, including the erection of a new ferry house and immigrant landing building at the far end of the ferry slip and new recreation buildings in the area between Islands Number 2 and Number 3, which had been filled in during the preceding decade. In the late 1930s the entire area was landscaped. Another New Deal project on the island was the beautification of some of the rooms. The Federal Art Project, part of the huge Works Progress Administration, employed out-of-work artists to paint a se-

When they did not find the pot of gold at the end of their journey to America, immigrants began yearning for their native lands again. To save the price of the passage back, some disillusioned newcomers resorted to anarchy; others manufactured evidence that they were undesirables. (Photo courtesy of UPI/Bettmann Newsphotos)

The Great Depression caused hardships for American citizens and immigrants alike. Although deportations eased some of the pressure on social institutions, it could not alleviate the problems. Unable to find work, these street urchins lived by their cunning and foraged for whatever food they could find amid the debris. At dusk their "pillow" might be a wooden wall, an empty barrel, or an older brother. (Photo courtesy of the Museum of the City of New York)

Under Commissioner Edward Corsi, deportation candidates were allowed daily, rather than twice weekly, visits. Detainees on Ellis Island could chat (behind a wall and security screen) with friends and relatives while waiting for a final decision. (Photo by Shirley C. Burden)

Commissioner Edward Corsi, once a settlement-house director, was faced with cleaning up Ellis Island. As part of that task he demolished the old canopy seen in the front of the main building. (Photo courtesy of the Theodore Koch Collection, Michigan Historical Collections, Bentley Historical Library, University of Michigan)

As part of the Works Progress Administration of the late 1930s, the Federal Art Project hired unemployed artists to paint a series of murals in the dining room. Painter Edward Laning and two assistants depicted immigrants toiling in American industries. This 1940s photo shows the part of the mural commemorating the construction of the transcontinental railway. (Photo courtesy of UPI/Bettmann Newsphotos)

During World War II Ellis Island harbored people suspected of not being sympathetic to America's war interest. Many of them were detained until global peace was declared. Conditions were not as favorable as when these detainees were escorted to the island in the 1950s. (Photo courtesy of the National Archives)

ries of huge murals on 110 feet of eight-foot-high wall space in the dining room. Executed by painter Edward Laning and two assistants, the murals, depicting immigrants working in American industries, were formally presented to the government in 1938.

Large-scale immigration to America returned briefly in September 1939, when war broke out in Europe. At about the same time, the United States Coast Guard, charged with the duty of protecting American neutrality, began to use part of the island as a training facility, taking over the new immigrant landing building and part of the baggage and dormitory building, which they continued to occupy until August 1946.

In 1940 the Immigration and Naturalization Service was transferred to the Justice Department, indicating the direction immigration policy had taken.

The goal of the Justice Department was to screen aliens rigorously since deportation was no longer an "efficacious means of protecting this country against that small percentage of aliens who prove unworthy of this country," according to the attorney general. Thus, he continued, "the immigrant to America came to be considered primarily in the aspect of his potential threat to the national security." New classes of aliens, including smugglers, illegal entrants to the country, and those who impaired the military forces in any way, were now subject to deportation.

When the United States entered the war in 1941, Ellis Island again served as a detention station for enemy aliens. Those aliens determined by the Immigration and Naturalization Service and the Federal Bureau of Investigation to be a threat to America's national security were held at stations around the country, including Ellis Island. Hundreds of Germans and Italians and some Japanese were interned on the island, many with their families, until they were released, sometimes on bond or their own recognizance, sometimes on parole. Many spent months awaiting hearings on their status. Hospitals on the island were again used as military facilities for returning servicemen. Major building renovations were made to the hospital complex during WWII.

Two pieces of legislation characterized the ambivalent feelings of Americans toward the outside world in the period after WWII. The first was the Displaced Persons Act of June 1948. Following President Harry S Truman's executive order of December 1945, more than forty thousand aliens were admitted to the United States as "displaced persons," victims of the war in Europe who had no homes when it ended. The act of 1948 extended this charitable action by granting visas to an additional 205,000 over a two-year period, a return to earlier American ideals about immigration and the United States as a land of opportunity.

The second act was a reflection of the national paranoia engendered by the cold war, the fall of China in 1949, and the outbreak of the Korean War in 1950. The Internal Security Act (or the McCarran Act) of September 1950 passed over Truman's veto. It sought to protect the United States from subversive (particularly communist) activities. The law barred

President Harry S Truman reopened the "golden door" by signing into law the Displaced Persons Act of June 1948. Victimized by the war, these people had no homes when peace was declared. (Photo courtesy of United Press International)

The 1948 act granted visas to an additional 205,000 immigrants who were displaced because of World War II. Once again the Statue of Liberty's beacon of freedom beckoned hundreds, like these shipboard immigrants, to her welcoming shore. (Photo © Dennis Stock, courtesy of Magnum Photos, Inc.)

Under the 1950 McCarran Act those suspected of Nazi or Fascist persuasion were held for screening at Ellis Island. In compliance with the new act, the U.S. Immigration and Naturalization Service sent 130 newcomers from the SS Saturnia *to Ellis Island. Eleanor Trice, the German-born wife of an American soldier, holds her daughter Maria during questioning by immigration officer Edward Ferro (seated), while Edward J. Shaughnessy, chief of the immigration service, peers over Ferro's shoulder. (Photo courtesy of UPI/Bettmann Newsphotos)*

all aliens who had been or were members of totalitarian organizations and provided for deportation of or denial of citizenship to such aliens already in the United States. This was followed in 1952 by the McCarran-Walter Act, a comprehensive new immigration law that contained the quota system established in 1924 and incorporated the internal security provisions of the 1950 McCarran Act. The attorney general and the Immigration and Naturalization Service were given new powers and responsibilities to strengthen enforcement procedures.

When the McCarran-Walter law took effect, it immediately lowered immigration figures, particularly the numbers who came through the Port of New York. It had relatively less effect at Ellis Island, however, since procedures adopted years earlier had already stemmed the flow of immigrants through the island. As early as 1942, Justice Department officials had discussed closing the island, since it was expensive to maintain and the administrative work done there could easily be transferred to offices at 70 Columbus Avenue, which the Immigration and Natural-ization Service had taken over from the defunct WPA.

By 1954 such arguments were unassailable. The buildings on the island were little used, as only two to three hundred immigrants were landed there at a time, and many of the closed buildings were dilapidated. One official estimated an annual savings of $800,000 to $900,000 would result from closing the island. Attorney General Herbert Brownell discussed his decision to close Ellis Island in a speech to thousands of newly naturalized citizens. After reviewing the island's glorious history, he observed: "But today the little island between the Statue of Liberty and the skyline and piers of New York seems to have served its purpose for immigration."

Without ceremony the island closed on Friday, November 12, 1954. The last detainee, Arne Peterssen, a Norwegian sailor who had missed his ship as it left port, was escorted from the island. Some furniture and equipment was transported to the offices on Columbus Avenue, and the island staff took its last ride to Battery Park aboard the ferryboat *Ellis Island*. An era had come to an end.

By the early 1950s Ellis Island facilities were rarely used. Only two to three hundred newcomers might wander between the ▶ graffiti-covered walls at a time; in fact, the U.S. Justice Department considered closing the island as early as 1947. Written by Greek immigrants in 1953, these messages reflect the stoicism of present and past newcomers to America's shores. The top work translates "the Cretan/No problem is without end/if you have patience." The middle work reads "the Fisherman from Hydra for a Woman/When your fate is to pass/from here, you will pass." The bottom message, written by a gentleman from northern Epirus, translates as "the old Latin saying says, dum spiro spero—/As long as I breathe, I hope." (Photo by Wilton S. Tifft)

In the 1950s detainees were provided an opportunity for physical exercise. Depicted here is the men's exercise yard, where detainees could stretch their legs, feed the pigeons, or just enjoy the sunshine. (Photo courtesy of the National Archives)

The federal government quietly closed the facilities on November 12, 1954, and the staff took their final ride across the harbor on the ferry Ellis Island. *Behind the bow (left) is Castle Garden. (Photo courtesy of the National Park Service)*

Empty but ready for the next bargeload of immigrants that would never come, this is the view from the east end of the registry room taken shortly after Ellis Island closed in 1954. It would be more than twenty years before this room would see regular traffic again. (Photo by Shirley C. Burden)

In an earlier era this food service line served hot meals on cold days to Ellis Island's many inspectors and examiners. The sizzle of pancakes on the griddle and the clang of ladles in the soup kettles were replaced over the years with the soft plop of falling paint chips. (Photo by Wilton S. Tifft)

In the recreation hall between Islands Number 2 and Number 3, the Coast Guard once blasted patriotic messages over the auditorium's loudspeaker system. The empty wooden seats remained at dress-command attention, though the curtain fell years before when the island closed. (Photo by Wilton S. Tifft)

Their native shoes stayed in silent homage to the Ellis Island experience, but the would-be Americans walked bravely into the New World as Ellis Island unceremoniously closed its doors. (Photo by Shirley C. Burden)

The ferryboat Ellis Island *gently rocked at berth shortly after the island's closing in 1954. (Photo by Shirley C. Burden)*

SEVEN

Limbo,
1954–1974

Little fanfare accompanied the closing of Ellis Island, but controversy was not long in coming. Throughout its history the little island had been the center of discussion and dissension, particularly since its selection as America's main immigration station. Now that it no longer served that purpose, the question became: what purpose should it serve? The answers were many and varied and engendered strong feelings.

The first concern was what to do with the aliens still detained on the island. Several dozen prospective immigrants and aliens awaiting deportation hearings under the McCarran Act were still on Ellis Island in early November. Of these, forty-six were transferred to nearby prisons.

Protest followed immediately. One of the leading protesters was Pearl S. Buck, the Nobel prize-winning author, who objected to the fact that "intelligent and good persons are treated as though they had committed crimes." Officials in the prisons where the detainees were held defended their institutions, but one woman who had been incarcerated took issue with them, citing the lack of decent reading material, fresh air, exercise, and contact with family members. "The transfer of detained aliens to jails—no matter what 'class'—hardly constitutes humane administration of immigration laws," she protested.

After a peculiar period of confusion in which the Justice Department and New York immigration authorities issued conflicting statements concerning whether any immigrants actually were in jail, district immigration director Edward O'Shaughnessy announced in early January 1955 that only a few immigrants were being housed in "dormitory" detention

◀ *Neglected and virtually abandoned for more than twenty years, this stone face above one of the first-floor windows seems to shed a sad tear. (Photo by Wilton S. Tifft)*

quarters in the old Federal Building at 641 Washington Street. None remained in local jails. For a while, at least, the question of what to do with detained aliens overshadowed the question of what to do with Ellis Island.

Once the fate of the detainees was settled, however, suggestions flew in rapidly. One of the first was that, since the island originally had been used by the Dutch for picnics, the circular theories of history would be charmingly served if the island were once again to become a picnic ground. One man suggested that a small airstrip for private planes could be built on the island. The New York State Department of Corrections indicated an interest, and an official who visited the site found the facilities impressive. Other New York state authorities considered its use for housing homeless men, delinquent boys, or chronic alcoholics. A New York businessman, L. R. Breslauer, proposed that the city establish an international trade center on the island and claimed to have received endorsements for the plan from thirteen foreign embassies.

Pointing out that Jersey City was only about a thousand feet from Ellis Island, state senator James F. Murray, Jr., spearheaded an effort for the Garden State to acquire the land for use as a cultural center and recreation area. One New Jersey public official suggested placing an ethnic museum on the island, citing "the great international symbolism implied in such a project." Soon afterward, the state legislature passed a resolution proposing that the United States government turn Ellis Island over to the state of New Jersey for educational and cultural purposes.

However, when the General Services Administration offered the island to Jersey City, New York City, and the states of New Jersey and New York, there were no takers. New York officials debated the possibility but recoiled from the costs. Besides the initial bid price for the island, valued in 1955 at $6.3 million,

Sixteen years after Ellis Island closed unceremoniously in 1954, the main building was already in a desolate state. The rooftop's decorative copper trim was dangling or missing from the east wing (left). While rust and decay marched forward, bureaucracy withheld a final decision on the former immigration station's status. (Photo by Wilton S. Tifft)

The registry room on the second floor looked as bleak as the battleground of Congress, where the disposition of Ellis Island was debated. Paint was chipping off the columns and the stair banister appeared quite worn. (Photo by Wilton S. Tifft)

Once 185 feet long, the neglected Edward Laning mural celebrating the construction of the transcontinental railway began disintegrating after the station closed. The remaining 35 feet were removed and restored in 1972; the mural now graces the federal courthouse in Brooklyn. (Photo by Wilton S. Tifft)

Tucked away in the cellar of the main building was an iron-mesh jail, which may have impressed officials from the New York Department of Corrections, who had indicated an interest in Ellis Island as a correctional facility. (Photo by Wilton S. Tifft)

The stairs were covered with the products of dilapidation and neglect, but the sun continued to shine through the Renaissance-arched window into the dormitory and baggage building. Decades earlier the New York Bible Society passed out "Godspeeds" and Good Books to newcomers at the foot of these stairs. (Photo by Wilton S. Tifft)

The walls and ceiling of the staff dining room were peeling away, but the chairs were placed neatly atop the tables, as if the sweeper would one day reclaim the broom in the lower right corner. (Photo by Wilton S. Tifft)

As the years passed and no use was found for the island's facilities, the dining room on the second floor of the main building fell into serious disrepair. (Photo by Wilton S. Tifft)

A solitary office chair sat beneath a broken skylight amid windblown debris in a versatile area of the main building. ▶
*During various periods this office hosted the Council of Jewish Women, housed the Bureau of Information, and served as
a waiting room for friends and relatives of immigrants. (Photo by Wilton S. Tifft)*

they estimated that maintenance costs would be at least $250,000 annually. In addition, most of the buildings were run-down and unusable in their present condition, a factor that would add millions to the cost. New Jersey officials had similar misgivings. Jersey City's mayor explained his loss of interest: "I had a lot of ideas about the island, but, frankly, after looking it over, I didn't see what we could do with it or what anyone else could do with it. It has massive, outdated buildings that would cost a fortune to heat. I think they would be good only for some kind of military installation."

Accordingly, the General Services Administration, the agency responsible for the disposal of surplus government property, decided to offer Ellis Island for sale to private developers at auction in September 1956. GSA newspaper ads declared that Ellis Island had the "perfect location and facilities for

Oil Storage Depot, Import and Export Processing, Warehousing, Manufacturing, Private Institutions, etc."

Controversy forestalled the sale of the island in 1956. While many public projects were proposed for Ellis Island, none was accompanied by adequate funding to restore or replace its old and dilapidated buildings. Nevertheless public sentiment strongly favored the government's retaining the island. At the urging of numerous political figures, President Dwight D. Eisenhower ordered the GSA to suspend the auction a week after its announcement. The president cited the need for time to study proposals for the island's public use and urged that such proposals be submitted to Congress for review.

Among the suggestions, one would continue to reappear from various sources. This was a plan for some sort of monument or shrine or museum com-

*Exposed to the elements by a broken skylight, a tree sprouted in the debris of one of the dining rooms in the dormitory
and baggage building. (Photo by Wilton S. Tifft)*

The discarded flag and ransacked desk were the only reminders left in a special inquiry examination room. While many public projects were suggested for Ellis Island, none came with the appropriate funding necessary to correct conditions in the dilapidated buildings. (Photo by Wilton S. Tifft)

Abandoned and neglected after Ellis Island closed, these tower stairs once witnessed a steady stream of immigrants, like the Slavic immigrants in 1905 (inset) who preferred to carry their belongings rather than trust them to the crowded baggage room on the first floor. (Photo by Wilton S. Tifft; inset photo by Lewis W. Hine, courtesy of the New York Public Library)

memorating the experience of the millions of immigrants who had passed through the Ellis Island station. No finer or more fitting use could have been chosen for Ellis Island, yet it took more than two decades to come to that decision. Aside from the usual dilatory nature of the federal bureaucracy, there were other reasons for the long delay in setting the island's future. One was the resistance provided by a group planning a similar "American Museum of Immigration" in the base of the Statue of Liberty. The vice chairman of the rival organization questioned the efficacy of a similar plan for Ellis Island:

[I]s Ellis Island the appropriate site for a tribute to immigration in the building of America? Agreed that this island provided the first physical contact with the United States for millions of immigrants, was it a place of inspiration for them, or was it not, for at least a substantial number of them, a painful and bewildering interlude in their adventure into a new life?

No immigrant was attracted to America by Ellis Island or by Castle Garden, which preceded it as a processing station for new arrivals. The lodestar for all of them was the torch of the Statue of Liberty. . . .

The proposals the government hoped to receive for Ellis Island never materialized. Cost was the major factor. By the end of 1957 a New York group estimated that, even if the city received the island as a gift from the federal government, the cost of just rehabilitating the buildings would be $1.8 million. Replacing the ferry service would cost an additional $1 million with annual operating costs of $210,000. Based on these figures, Ellis Island would be too dear a gift to accept.

Having exhausted the alternatives for public use, the GSA once again offered the island at a public auction in January 1958, with sealed bids to be submitted and opened on February 14. Yet even as the GSA awaited bids, new proposals came forth. The most unusual was from Congressman Paul A. Fino of New York, who suggested the island be used for a national lottery center—"the national site for the legalized gambling spirit of the American people whose ancestors gambled for a new life in this land of ours."

[150]

Only a few items of furniture were left in this first-floor medical examination room where men and boys once anxiously waited for their turn with the doctor (inset). (Photo by Wilton S. Tifft; inset photo courtesy of the National Park Service)

The high bidder in the auction was a New York builder, Sol G. Atlas, who bid $201,000 for the island and its buildings. Atlas planned to raze all the Ellis Island buildings and erect a $55 million resort and cultural center. His "Pleasure Island" complex would include a resort hotel, a convention center, a museum, tennis courts, and a gigantic outdoor movie screen adjacent to a marina, where moviegoers would watch in boats rather than automobiles. In early April the government rejected all the bids for Ellis Island, claiming they were all too low for the property, now valued at $6,326,000.

In 1959 and again in 1960 the government solicited bids at auction for the island. In both cases the high bidder was Sol Atlas, who still planned to develop Pleasure Island there. Again, in both cases, the GSA rejected the bids as too low, although Atlas's 1960 bid was for $1,025,000. The real problem seems not to have been the amount of money offered but the purpose to which the island should be devoted. Each time the government offered Ellis Island for public sale to private interests, an unspoken feeling seemed to arise that this was a place of special significance,

never to be sold at any price. To the millions of living immigrants who had passed through the station, and to their tens of millions of descendants, it seemed almost sacrilegious to allow such an important place—an isle of hopes as well as tears—to be sold off to commercial developers. The symbolic value of Ellis Island outweighed its mere property value.

In the early 1960s redesigning the island became a challenge to architects and architectural students. Cooper Union students collaborated on an idealistic model of a research center for peacetime applications of nuclear energy, which fit the dimensions of the island. The buildings they envisioned included a twenty-two-story apartment/administration building, research laboratories, an exhibition hall, a library, an auditorium, and a nuclear reactor. Pratt Institute held a competition for designs for Ellis Island. The winning plans included an international trade center, a nautical museum, and a "United Nations of Religion." Even the late Frank Lloyd Wright entered the picture. In 1962 two NBC television staffers proposed to build a "Dream City" based on tower and dome drawings sketched for Ellis Island by the famous ar-

The rooms in the east and west wings of the main building served different functions at different times. This medical examination room on the first floor might have been used, at another time, as a two-story vault housing the documentation of the immigrants who passed through Ellis Island. Years later all that remained were the privacy shields, an examination table, and the doctors' old medical cabinets. (Photo by Wilton S. Tifft)

Ellis Island was self-contained. This boiler room supplied the electricity for equipment and lighting as well as the steam for heating the buildings on Ellis Island. (Photo by Wilton S. Tifft)

This arched window was mirror-imaged by a pool of water, not a waxed shine on the tile floor. (Photo by Shirley C. Burden)

In the Office of Special Inquiry an ornate safe was left with its decorative doors open. Surrounded by fallen plaster, wooden moldings, and a lost roll of toilet paper, it was once used to guard detained immigrants' valuables. (Photo by Wilton S. Tifft)

Washed but still damp hospital sheets were hand-fed into this mangle, which dried and ironed them under a series of hot rollers in one step. Finished sheets were caught and hand-folded at the exit end. (Photo by Wilton S. Tifft)

chitect shortly before his death in 1959.

In the summer of 1960 a group of well-known educators, including Harry Carman, dean emeritus of Columbia University, Lewis Webster Jones, former president of Rutgers University, and notable professors such as Mark Van Doren, Seymour Harris, Clinton Rossiter, Arthur M. Schlesinger, Jr., and Eric Goldman, announced plans for a "college of the future" on the island. Start-up money remained an insurmountable obstacle, however, and the "college of the future" languished.

Several proposals to use the island for educational or welfare purposes came before the Department of Health, Education, and Welfare for review, but all were ultimately rejected as unsuitable or lacking clear funding prospects.

The alternative plan, which kept reappearing, was the national immigration monument idea. In the early 1960s a leading proponent of this plan was former commissioner of immigration Edward Corsi. With historians Allan Nevins and Oscar Handlin, Corsi organized the American Council for Nationalities Service, which endorsed the operation of Ellis Island by the National Park Service "as a park for educational and recreational purposes, and part of it used for exhibits and displays." The council characterized an Ellis Island museum as an "extension" of

This fireproof corridor connected the buildings on Islands Number 2 and Number 3. The wooden plank roof protected travelers from the outside elements, and during evening hours ceiling fixtures lit the way to the laundry building and hospital complex on Island Number 2. (Photo by Wilton S. Tifft)

This is the shirts and pants ironing area of the laundry room. The item to be pressed was placed on the asbestos-lined board; the operator then grasped the ironing bar with both hands and pulled it down to press the garment. Once the operator released the bar, it ascended to its original position and the pressed item could be removed. (Photo by Wilton S. Tifft)

the American Museum of Immigration on Liberty Island. Foremost in their reasoning was that Ellis Island be preserved as a public place—"a visual reminder of an important part of our American heritage and as an instrument for perpetuating the democratic faith of the many different peoples who have found a new life in America and who have joined in building its greatness."

Three-and-a-half years of studies, commissions, and intergovernmental meetings ensued. The government vacillated between public uses of the island, which did not meet necessary funding requirements, and sale to private interests for development. What may have ultimately decided the issue was the influential support given to the idea of using the island for an immigration monument. In September 1963 Senator Edmund Muskie of Maine suggested integrating Ellis Island with Liberty Island and the proposed waterfront development of Jersey City, with all three areas to be managed by the National Park Service. New York mayor Robert F. Wagner and Senator Jacob Javits of New York endorsed the plan, as did the American Institute of Architects.

The Department of the Interior announced its plan in mid-June 1964. Liberty Island and Ellis Island would both display material on American immigration, with the museum on Ellis Island devoted to the later phase of the migration in the late nineteenth and early twentieth centuries. Jersey City would donate eighty-eight acres of waterfront property for the partial development of a five-hundred-acre park, to be linked via a causeway to Ellis Island. The dilapidated buildings on the island would be razed, with only those of great historical interest retained.

After several months of planning and a recommendation from Interior Secretary Stewart Udall, President Lyndon B. Johnson officially designated Ellis Island part of the Statue of Liberty National Monument on May 11, 1965. In a speech he made at the time of the formal resolution, Johnson noted that much of the rehabilitation work on Ellis Island and in Liberty State Park along the nearby New Jersey coast would be undertaken by youths working in the Job Corps, one of the administration's agencies designated to fight the "war on poverty" in America. Congress appropriated $6 million for the development of the island, which President Johnson approved in August.

An early institutional drum washer was used to sanitize hospital linens. Even with all this equipment still in place, the 27.5 acres of Ellis Island brought a high bid of only $201,000 at auction in 1958, so the government rejected all bids. (Photo by Wilton S. Tifft)

Among the now-antique equipment abandoned in the laundry building, this early cast-iron model of the spin dryer, known as an "extractor," waited patiently for more hospital linens to fluff. (Photo by Wilton S. Tifft)

New York architect Philip Johnson was commissioned to redesign Ellis Island. Johnson, who had previously planned the New York State Theater at Lincoln Center and a new wing of the Museum of Modern Art, submitted his plans early the following year. The centerpiece of his sketches was a hollow concrete tower 130 feet high, which the architect dubbed "The Wall of the Sixteen Million." All along the wall, to be ascended by visitors on special ramps, Johnson planned to place plaques bearing the names of immigrants who had entered America through Ellis Island. In the center of the structure he included a pool a hundred feet in diameter, around which statues might be placed. The plan also called for the preservation of the old main building and hospital complex. These buildings would be structurally stabilized, with no interior restoration, and with glass and wood removed from the exteriors. Vines would be allowed to grow on these "stabilized ruins," as visitors pondered what the island must have been like when immigrants were ushered through the buildings. The intention was to create a sense of nostalgia and romance rather than to meticulously reconstruct the physical artifacts.

Secretary Udall praised the design as a blend of "art and architecture and history" and estimated its completion in eight to ten years at a cost of $12 million. An architectural critic who assessed the plan concluded, "It is light-years ahead of the routine reconstructions and predictably pedestrian memorials usually tendered by government agencies."

But like many of the dreams of the mid-1960s, the grandiose visions for Ellis Island were lost in the quagmire of United States military involvement in Southeast Asia. The Vietnam War assumed a priority in the funding programs of the later years of the

> *"[After the closing in 1954] . . . they let it fall down. It was a shame because we had built it up to such a beautiful place. Prior to that we had painted the whole place, always kept it clean, always up to date. We had the most gorgeous grounds that you could want. They called it a country club. The passengers themselves, or I should say, the aliens themselves."*
> —Louis Sillen, worked in the Boarding Division on Ellis Island during WWII and after

Johnson administration. Funds appropriated for other projects, like Ellis Island, were rechanneled, and the projects were shelved and forgotten. A visitor to Ellis Island in March 1968 found that the island was "pretty much at its low point in history." The ferryboat *Ellis Island* was deteriorating, as was the concrete dock to which it was attached. The interior of the main building was covered with "a blanket of grime," and fallen ceiling plaster lay everywhere. The entire island resembled "a seedy ghost town."

As the Johnson plan for Ellis Island became an orphan of war, the National Park Service developed its own less ambitious plan to develop the island for visitors. This proposal, approved in November 1968, emphasized preservation rather than new construction and called for the retention of the main building, the ferryboat *Ellis Island*, and the covered walkways. All other buildings were to be removed, except for "three relatively modern buildings temporarily retained for use pending completion of development."

Even this modest proposal suffered from a lack of funding. Except for some minor repairs to the main building (most notably to the roof), little was effected during the rest of the decade. As if to symbolize the plight of Ellis Island, the ferryboat of the same name sank at her berth in August 1968. Originally commissioned in a shipyard in Wilmington, Delaware, in 1904, when Miss Mabel Sargent, daughter of Commissioner General of Immigration Frank B. Sargent, broke a bottle of champagne on her hull, the *Ellis Island* had logged an estimated one million miles in fifty years of service. Buried at the bottom of a list of budget priorities for years, she now lay buried under tons of water in the ferry slip.

Like the submerged ship, the island lay dormant

The mental health facility on Ellis Island was Ward 13. On the right-hand door frame was the buzzer, which would alert an attendant to allow the Ward 13 visitor entrance. (Photo by Wilton S. Tifft)

After Ellis Island was officially designated part of the Statue of Liberty National Monument, proposals were made to tear down the buildings on the south half of the island. However, the cost of the Vietnam War limited available funds, and contagious diseases Ward 24 remained standing. This photograph now hangs as a mural on permanent display in the Ellis Island Immigration Museum. (Photo by Wilton S. Tifft)

[163]

Some immigrants survived the journey only to succumb to illness before setting foot in the New World, and, occasionally, someone denied entrance preferred death to the return trip. All rested temporarily in Ellis Island's morgue (pictured here) awaiting disposition of the remains. (Photo by Wilton S. Tifft)

as an item of governmental concern until 1970, when a group of militant Native Americans sought to emulate another Indian group's occupation of Alcatraz a few months earlier by taking over Ellis Island. Setting out from the New Jersey coast just before dawn on March 16, 1970, eight men planned to ferry a boatload of equipment and thirty other Indians to the island before federal authorities could take notice and intervene. Their launch broke down in mid-channel, however, and the Coast Guard arrived before the engine could be repaired. A spokesman for the Indians stated that their plan was to use the island as

A laundry cart continued to wait for the soiled linens of a busier era in the corridor along the contagious diseases wards of Island Number 3. (Photo by Wilton S. Tifft)

a center of Indian culture, where displays could demonstrate what white people had given the Native Americans—"disease, alcohol, poverty, and cultural desecration."

In spite of increased Coast Guard vigilance, a few months later another group succeeded in occupy-

ing the island. On July 20 sixty-four members of the National Economic Growth and Reconstruction Organization (NEGRO) moved quietly to Ellis Island. Their announced purpose was to demonstrate that "society's forgotten, drug addicts, multigeneration welfare recipients, and former prison inmates" could

The modern lines of twentieth-century architecture were featured in the new ferry house, built in 1934 at the end of the ferry slip. (Photo by Wilton S. Tifft)

These benches on the ferryboat Ellis Island *undoubtedly carried many immigrants to New York City on their way to their future homes, but after years of idleness the paint on the rafters peeled away. Eventually the saltwater and salt-saturated air took their ultimate toll, and the ferryboat sank in its slip. (Photo by Wilton S. Tifft)*

Two lifeboats, capable of saving twenty-one immigrants, could not save their ferryboat Ellis Island. ▶
(Photo by Wilton S. Tifft)

© 1986 Wilton S. Tifft

Looking from inside the ferry building in 1983, the old ferry slip and the remains of the ferryboat Ellis Island *can be seen in the foreground. In the background, scaffolding has gone up around the main building. The renovation had begun. (Photo by Wilton S. Tifft)*

"create a self-supporting, productive, rehabilitative community." The group called its takeover "an act of friendly seizure" and pledged to leave the island in a few days.

NEGRO sought a permit from the National Park Service to develop the island as a rehabilitation center where former addicts and convicts could be trained to work in other businesses owned by the group. During their twelve-day stay on the island, group members demonstrated the potential of their idea by converting the old ferry building into a factory where chemicals were packaged, under a preexisting contract with the federal government.

The National Park Service granted a five-year special-use permit for Ellis Island to NEGRO in September 1970. The organization pledged to develop a rehabilitation center for twenty-five hundred former addicts, convicts, and their families. The group also planned to develop the island for tourists, display historical exhibits, and work with various ethnic groups on celebrations and programs, such as inviting people of Irish descent to celebrate St. Patrick's Day on the island. The costs engendered in rehabilitating the physical facilities would be paid by visitors

and by the operation of factories on the island.

This worthy-sounding plan failed, as had its predecessors. NEGRO did not prove to be financially stable and vacated the island. In the spring of 1973 the National Park Service revoked its permit to NEGRO on the grounds of "health and safety."

For most of the two decades after the immigration station closed on Ellis Island, the place was deserted. Other than an occasional visit by officials from some agency or other, only a daytime watchman (and a few nighttime vandals) disturbed the quietude. The brick buildings slowly decayed, and underbrush and weeds crept stealthily over the old walkways. A solitary photographer roamed the ruins some days, recording the devastation, but otherwise the place was as deserted as it had been four hundred years earlier, when the gulls had made it their home to feast on oysters in the bay.

However, the war in Vietnam was winding down, the Bicentennial of the United States was approaching, and a sense of history's importance was being instilled in the populace. Plans were being made.

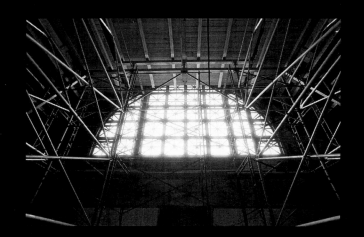

EIGHT

Restoration and Renovation, 1974–1990

With the approach of the Bicentennial, interest in Ellis Island resurfaced, and once again its fate was debated among various groups. As it was in the past, the key to Ellis Island's own future was money. The buildings had so deteriorated by the middle of the decade that the $6 million authorized (but never fully appropriated) by Congress ten years earlier fell far short of what was needed to develop the site. Estimates now ranged from several million dollars up to $70 million. Raising such an amount seemed absolutely impossible. The solution was to start small.

Among those wanting to restore Ellis Island during the 1970s was Dr. Peter Sammartino, chancellor and founder of Fairleigh Dickinson University in Rutherford, New Jersey. The son of Italian immigrant parents who journeyed through Ellis Island, Sammartino was chairman of the International Committee of the New Jersey Bicentennial Commission. He proposed that the state commission undertake fixing up Ellis Island, razing all but the main building which could be refurbished as a museum for tourists.

In 1974 the Restore Ellis Island Committee was created, with Sammartino at its head. This committee along with others lobbied Congress for funds to rehabilitate Ellis Island in order to reopen the island in time for the Bicentennial. Their efforts paid off and on January 1, 1976, President Gerald Ford signed an appropriation bill granting $1 million to fix up the main building and $500,000 to the NPS to run the site.

Once the initial funding was authorized, NPS officials worked quickly to make the main building safe for visitors. Plans for dredging the ferry basin were put on hold for lack of money, but workers cleared rubble and prepared walkways and a landing area for tourists.

Work was completed in May 1976, and Ellis Island was officially reopened to the public on May 28, following a ceremony the day before attended by politicians and officials of the groups involved in the work. Visitors arrived at Ellis Island via a ferryboat that left six times daily from Liberty Island. Once there, tourists walked through the deteriorated facilities on a one-hour tour led by Park Service rangers that traced the route of immigrants through the main building, where immigrant processing took place.

By September tour boats were also scheduled daily from Liberty State Park in New Jersey to Ellis Island. While the tours were discontinued in the winter months, they resumed the following May.

The tours continued in subsequent years, but so did the deterioration of the island, for the amount authorized each year by Congress was insufficient to make any but minor repairs. The National Park Service initiated an "Analysis of Alternatives" to identify and study various ways to accomplish a major restoration and renovation of the site. Meanwhile, *New York Times* writer Sidney H. Schanberg, addressing the problem in July 1981, noted that the mention of Ellis Island conjured up visions of a romantic, nostalgic place, whereas in fact "Ellis Island now is about as romantic as a row of hollow buildings in the South Bronx." The one building open for tourists was the main building, Schanberg reported, but it was in sad condition:

This one had been shored up and rendered safe, but it is moldering. Interior walls have crumbled. Mounds of fallen plaster and pools of rainwater from leaking roofs spread darkly across some of the floors. Dust and peeling paint are the most benign signs of the slow rot. Windows are out, and in one room moss and small trees are grow-

◀ *Light from the arched window at the east end of the Great Hall (registry room) streams through scaffolding erected to enable workers to inspect and repair tiles in the vaulted ceiling during restoration. (Photo by Wilton S. Tifft)*

A wheelchair was left overturned in front of the main building. Over a side entrance, the ornate copper frieze wearily drooped in desperate testimony to the need for rehabilitation. This photo now hangs as a mural on permanent display in the Elllis Island Immigration Museum. (Photo by Wilton S. Tifft)

ing, and pigeons have settled in. Here and there bits of salvaged old furniture have been arranged forlornly in an attempt to recapture the era.

Schanberg suggested the possibility of a public fund-raising effort to restore Ellis Island, a project the National Park Service had estimated would cost between $75 and $100 million. In fact, the Department of the Interior was already considering a public-private partnership in connection with raising funds to restore the Statue of Liberty in time for her centennial in 1986. The advantage of such a relationship was twofold. First, the money for such a project would come from private donations rather than government funds. Second, management of the construction project would be the responsibility of the private sector, thus enabling the work to be done more quickly than if under government control.

In 1982 Interior Secretary James Watt approached Lee Iacocca about heading such a public-private partnership for the Statue. At that time, Iacocca, whose own parents had come through Ellis Island, suggested including Ellis Island in the project. Some years earlier, Iacocca had been asked by a group of investors to put funds into developing a real estate project on the island. Appalled that this historic spot was being considered for such use, he refused. By adding Ellis Island to the fund-raising drive for the Statue, he saw a way to ensure the future of Ellis Island as a historic monument. A group of prominent Americans was appointed to the Statue of Liberty–Ellis Island Centennial Commission in May 1982 and in naming Iaccoca to head the Commission, President Ronald Reagan spoke of the significance of recognizing America's immigrants:

> I can't help but believe—you can call it mysticism, if you will—that God must have placed this land here between the two oceans to be found by a certain kind of people, that whatever corner of the world they came from they had the courage and the desire for freedom that went with it to uproot themselves and come to this strange land.

The commission was to serve as the primary citizen advisory body to the Department of the Interior and the National Park Service on all matters relating to the restoration and preservation of both the Statue of Liberty and Ellis Island. Initially the

The Guastavino tile work on the vaulted ceiling and the Boring & Tilton–designed brass and glass chandeliers were restored. Restoration workers tested each of the 28,282 buff-colored dovetailed tiles, repairing some and replacing only 17 of them. (Photo by Wilton S. Tifft)

commission aimed to raise $230 million to complete work on the Statue of Liberty by its centennial in 1986 and on Ellis Island by its 1992 centennial. (This figure would later change several times and by early 1990 almost $400 million had been raised for the two monuments.) However, its charter did not allow the commission to actually solicit money, so an agreement was signed with a nonprofit organization designed specifically for fund-raising purposes.

The Statue of Liberty–Ellis Island Foundation, Inc., was assigned the responsibility of raising the needed funds and contracting for construction. Iacocca would work closely with the foundation, eventually assuming its chairmanship as well in September 1984.

While the commission was advisory in nature and the foundation existed for the purpose of fund-raising and managing the construction, the National Park Service was charged with approving all plans for the restoration. In September 1982 NPS announced its own "General Management Plan," which detailed the way the restoration project would be

In May 1984 plans to restore the two-story Great Hall, along with the rest of the main building and powerhouse, to its 1918–1924 condition were announced. The staircase to the third floor balcony in the background was built when the Coast Guard used the facility and would have to be removed. (Photo by Wilton S. Tifft)

In September 1986 a plan to save the south half of Ellis Island for its architectural and sentimental merits was approved. Seen here are the newly cleaned hospital and administration buildings on Island Number 2. (Photo by Wilton S. Tifft)

managed and defined the overall objectives of the Ellis Island restoration:

1. To preserve the Ellis Island complex and return the buildings to active life by devoting major historic structures to public use and interpretation and by making the contributing structures available for adaptive use
2. To preserve the interiors of the major historic structures on Ellis Island and, through tours and programs, recall the human drama that occurred within these walls and explore the far-reaching effects it had on our nation
3. To preserve the thousands of artifacts that are extant on Ellis Island and those that have been donated by families of immigrants to develop a collection that will record and help convey the Ellis Island story

The plan encouraged cooperation between government agencies and private enterprises. The island was to be divided into two zones: the northern part of the island, which contained the most historically significant buildings on Ellis Island, was designated for "preservation/interpretation." Work on this zone would be completed by 1992, the centennial of the monument, and would be paid for by funds raised by the Foundation.

The southern part of the island, containing sup-port buildings, was marked for "adaptive use" and would be developed and funded by private organizations in a special arrangement with the National Park Service. It was this part of the plan that would later become the center of a storm of controversy about the private use of a historic site.

From the beginning the fund-raising program was a smooth-sailing operation. The Statue of Liberty–Ellis Island Foundation established headquarters in New York City, with affiliate offices in Chicago, Atlanta, Dallas, and Los Angeles. Its initial effort was an appeal to the American public through the mail. In addition the Foundation, under the direction of its chief operating officer Steve Briganti, began to solicit corporate sponsorships. In return for large pledges ($5 million or more in some cases) sponsors were permitted to use the official logo of the Foundation in their advertising, thus connecting their products with a patriotic cause. Charitable foundations were also approached, and more than two hundred responded with cash grants for unspecified use or with gifts designated specifically for Ellis Island, such as $1 million from the William Randolph Hearst Foundation and $500,000 from the Ford Foundation.

The Foundation also raised smaller amounts through its grass-roots campaign, which was launched on July 4, 1984. Ethnic organizations, ser-

The baggage room also was reclaimed by the renovation plans. (Photo by Wilton S. Tifft)

vice clubs, and business and civic organizations in cities and towns across the nation were encouraged to sponsor events whose proceeds would be donated for the restoration of the Statue of Liberty and Ellis Island. One of the Foundation's press releases listed examples of fund-raising activities in various locales: "Bake sales, auctions, raffles, jog-a-thons, dances, dinners, sports outings, direct solicitation of members, and treasury gifts." Not only did these groups contribute money they had raised, but many with former immigrants as members also contributed artifacts related to immigration and oral history interviews. As the Foundation noted, the grass-roots campaign also achieved one other goal, perhaps the most important: "namely, to evoke the commitment, support, and participation of a broad cross-section of the American public."

Supporting the fund-raising efforts was an estimated $150 million worth of free advertising in all media soliciting donations for the Statue of Liberty and Ellis Island, due to the efforts of the Advertising Council, Inc., from 1983 to 1989. The Ad Council distributed the public service ads to various television and radio stations, newspapers, and magazines which ran the material for free. Included in the campaign were public service announcements by Gregory Peck, a "Peanuts" television commercial by cartoonist Charles Schulz, a series of eighteen free ads run by

Time, and a special promotion for The American Immigrant Wall of Honor.

After the initial fund-raising efforts began, the National Park Service hired two architectural firms to collaborate on the project. Beyer Blinder Belle of New York City was best known for its work in historic preservation, while the Boston firm of Anderson Notter Finegold (which became Notter Finegold & Alexander) specialized in integrating modern facilities with historic buildings. Architect Michael Adlerstein was the NPS project director. He was later succeeded by Richard Wells.

Work on Ellis Island was centered on the main building, the most important structure on the island. It was here that the immigrants—twelve million in all—were processed before being allowed to enter America.

Flanked by four brick and limestone towers, the building was a deserted mausoleum trapped behind double twelve-foot chain-linked fencing when the restoration crews arrived in the fall of 1983. The fences, installed when Ellis Island served mostly as a detention center, were armed with barbed wire and electrical insulators. Elevated watchtowers that had been placed strategically around the site during World War II still stood.

Renovation plans for the main building, in the center of which was the two-story registry room or

James Rossant's design for the southern half of the island called for the restoration and reconversion of more than thirty buildings into a hotel and conference center. National Park Service officials favored the concept to bring new life and use to Ellis Island. This view from Island Number 2 shows a lone birch tree, spared by the brush-clearing. Later, however, the tree was felled to open the site. (Photo by Wilton S. Tifft)

Great Hall, were announced at a news conference in May 1984. The ambitious program included the total refurbishing of the hall and construction of a hundred-thousand-square-foot immigration museum in the building along with a library, an oral history room, two theaters, and a special learning center. The plan also called for the building of a wide staircase in the Great Hall. The original stairs—where the newcomers received their first perfunctory medical inspection—were initially located in the center of the hall, then moved to the east end, and finally dismantled. Since no photographs or blueprints of these historic stairs could be found, the architects designed a contemporary staircase at the east end of the Great Hall.

The work on Ellis Island soon became one of the largest restoration projects in the history of the United States, with approximately $160 million devoted to the preparation of the northern part of the island. The Foundation appointed Larry Bellante of GSGSB as the project director to supervise the activities of the Foundation's construction management company, Lehrer McGovern Bovis. The first task was to dry out the main building, which had been left unheated and exposed to the elements for decades. This twelve- to eighteen-month process was followed by demolition, structural work to adapt the building

to its new use, installation of modern mechanical systems, interior repair of floor tiles, scrubbing of white-glazed wall tiles, and replastering of parts of the upper walls to simulate Caen stone stucco. The dominant feature of the registry room, the high vaulted ceiling built by the Guastavino brothers in 1918, was in remarkably good shape. Restoration workers tested each of the 28,282 tiles for soundness and fit and had to replace only seventeen tiles. Two huge brass and glass chandeliers, designed by the building's architects, Boring & Tilton, were restored. The third is a reproduction.

The exterior of the building was a monument to the ravages of time. Scaffolding was erected around the structure for work on the brick facade and the decorative limestone trim. The roof was restored by removing the red tiles and rebuilding the wooden inner roof. Enough original tiles were undamaged to cover the main roof, but these included tiles from the six dormer windows that lighted the Great Hall. New tiles, chosen to match the originals, were used for the dormer roofs. The copper of the original domes and spires atop the towers on the main building was long gone when restoration started, so new globes and spires were hand-fabricated. The spires were then set in place with the use of a helicopter. The iron canopy that had led to the main entrance of the building

Fifteen years after the island closed, the grounds were quite overgrown. In summer the leaves of the many saplings that had taken root would have hidden both the hospital administration building (left) and the main building across the ferry slip (center). (Photo by Wilton S. Tifft)

As the scaffolding went up in the 1980s and workers began the restoration of the main building, other workers began clearing away the brush from the recreation area between Islands Number 2 and Number 3. (Photo by Wilton S. Tifft)

In early 1990 the grounds look as neat and fresh as the fully restored main building. (Photo by Wilton S. Tifft)

from 1903 to the 1930s was replaced by a modern glass-and-steel structure. The main entrance itself, which had been closed in the 1940s and its doors replaced by thirty-foot windows, was also restored.

To facilitate construction work on the island the Foundation erected a structure that people had been discussing since the 1890s but that had never materialized—a bridge from New Jersey to Ellis Island. This Bailey-type bridge (named after the British engineer who invented the structure for use during World War II) was a temporary structure 1,360 feet long and twenty-four feet wide made up of seven-foot sections of galvanized steel. Although it cost $2.1 million to build, one writer estimated that it might save as much as $20 million in the cost of transporting material to and from the island.

As the restoration of the buildings took shape, so did plans for the exhibits. Under the direction of Gary G. Roth, NPS project manager for the museum, a team of exhibit designers, producers, historians, conservators, and others began working to turn the main building into a world-class museum.

The development of the museum began with the preparation of an "Interpretive Prospective" by the National Park Service. They then selected three firms—MetaForm, a leading design and communications group, and two major exhibit producers, Rathe Productions and D&P—to collaborate in designing and fabricating the museum. Throughout the process the collaborative worked closely with members of a special history committee established by the Centennial Commission as well as with other immigration experts to create themes for various exhibits.

It was decided that renovated spaces in the east and west wings would hold displays documenting the Ellis Island story and the peak years of immigration—1880 to 1924—while the railroad ticket office would contain graphic displays of immigration statistics.

As the exhibit designs took shape, a nationwide appeal was launched for immigration-related artifacts that would augment the National Park Service's own collection. Hundreds of people, including immigrants and their descendants, retired Ellis Island workers, and collectors, responded.

Along with this appeal the National Park Service conducted another kind of search for relics of Ellis Island. Beginning in the summer of 1983 a group of museum studies students at New York University, under the supervision of the National Park Service, began exploring the island for artifacts to be selectively preserved. Early finds in and around the buildings included furniture, dishes, radios, identification cards, record books, and graffiti scribbled on the walls in a dozen different languages. Twenty-five areas were selected for preservation. During excavations for utilities in the basement of the main building, the skeletal remains of three individuals, determined to be Native Americans, were uncovered. Ceremonies to resanctify the ground took place in 1987, and the remains were reinterred prior to opening the museum. Digging on the island also uncovered many artifacts associated with Manhattan around the turn of the century, a fact that lent credence to the theory that much of the island's landfill had come from Manhattan when subways were being built there. As one park service official observed, "Digging through Ellis Island, we find old Manhattan."

While work was proceeding steadily on the northern half of the island, the southern part, designated for adaptive use, became the center of controversy. The National Park Service had sponsored a competition for the use of the area, which William Hubbard, president of the nonprofit Center for Housing Partnerships, won with a plan designed by James Rossant. The plan called for the restoration and adaptive use of more than thirty buildings as a hotel and conference center. Hubbard's original plan called for leasing the hotel facilities to a private concern and extending tax incentives to builders involved in the project. The plan also included tennis courts, swimming pools, a health center, and a marina. National Park Service officials generally favored this adaptive approach, which would save the island's original buildings, but hesitated about the tennis courts, swimming pools, health center, and marina. Some members of the Centennial Commission, and Lee Iacocca in particular, wanted to look at other options.

Some of the red roofing tiles had been damaged or were missing from the original roof. Additional tiles were removed to repair the wooden subroof, which was seriously damaged. Workers then replaced the original tiles wherever possible. The new skylight floods the museum area with sunlight. (Photo by Wilton S. Tifft)

John Burgee, a member of the Centennial Commission's architecture and engineering subcommittee, also submitted a couple of plans calling for an "ethnic Williamsburg" on the southern island. His first plan called for razing the buildings and replacing them with a large glass structure of his own design. When this plan proved unacceptable, Burgee submitted a second plan that proposed adaptive use of the existing historic structures.

The sometimes-heated debate over the best use of the southern part of the island continued throughout 1985 and into 1986.

In the middle of this controversy Interior Secretary Donald P. Hodell added fuel to the fire when he

After work was completed on the brick-and-limestone towers, they were ready for the eleven-foot copper domes. Handworked by artisans, the metal ornamentation and sheathing reproduced the originals. (Photo by Wilton S. Tifft)

"fired" Lee Iacocca as chairman of the Centennial Commission on February 12, 1986. Hodell seemed concerned that, since Iacocca headed both the Foundation, which had raised the money, and the Commission, which had approved the plans to spend that money, some might construe the situation as a conflict of interest. Hodell decided that Iacocca could chair either the Commission or the Foundation but not both. Iacocca chose the Foundation, although he protested that he should have some say in how the money was spent. As chairman of the Foundation which raised the money, he felt strongly that the Foundation was accountable to the public who so generously gave to the project.

With Iacocca gone from the Commission, the architectural subcommittee finally approved a compromise of the Center for Housing Partnerships' plan in September 1986. Purged of its marina, swimming pools, health center, tennis courts, and commercial hotel management, the plan now was for an international conference center managed by area universities—a facility comparable to those at Versailles, France, and Geneva, Switzerland. "Central to their report," according to the *New York Times*, "was the concept that the buildings should be preserved for their architectural merit and that the statue [of Liberty] and the Great Hall more than convey the themes of liberty and immigration."

Before disbanding and with reservations from its finance committee, the entire commission approved the conference center plan in June 1987, and what had been the center of controversy soon took a backseat to the long-awaited opening of the northern half of Ellis Island in the fall of 1990—almost a year and a half ahead of schedule.

As visitors today relive the experiences of the seventeen million immigrants who walked through Ellis Island before them on the way to a new life, they may share the sentiment of Henry James, who visited Ellis Island shortly after the turn of the century and was profoundly affected by the experience. He wrote: "I think indeed that the simplest account of the action of Ellis Island on the spirit of any sensitive citizen who may have happened to 'look in' is that he comes back from his visit not at all the same person that he went."

Once the copper dome was completed, a helicopter was used to hoist each fifteen-hundred-pound spire atop the dome. Like the domes, the spires were handcrafted by artisans. (Photo by Wilton S. Tifft)

Scaffolding removed and fully assembled, the tower's new finial glistens in the sunlight. (Photo by Wilton S. Tifft)

Immigrants walked under a covered walkway from the landing to the front steps of the main building. The original walkway was gone, but a contemporary glass canopy suggests its older, departed counterpart. (Photo by Wilton S. Tifft)

Visitors to today's Ellis Island can view four main exhibit areas that together make them the third-largest museum in New York. The museum also houses two theaters, galleries for rotating exhibits, an immigration library, and The American Immigrant Wall of Honor. (Photo by Wilton S. Tifft)

In the summer of 1983 New York University archaeology students scoured Ellis Island for artifacts to be preserved by the National Park Service for museum displays. Some of these pots, pans, and pitchers in the cellar were saved because they helped feed thousands of immigrants. (Photo by Wilton S. Tifft)

An Architectural Walk-Through

by James W. Rhodes, AIA

Beyer Blinder Belle/Notter Finegold & Alexander Inc.

For nearly three decades Ellis Island silently deteriorated. By the winter of 1983, when the architectural advance team arrived on Ellis Island, they were dismayed to find sections of the main building almost buried beneath drifts of snow, ice, and debris. Erosion of this premier example of the French Renaissance design period was very apparent.

Damage also was insidiously concealed in rooms where artifacts, building components, and rubbish were thrown together. The restoration team's task was to sort through the dilapidation for the historically important items that should be saved.

Following several years of detailed research and study by the National Park Service along with consulting architects and engineers, the restoration plans were drawn. Work focused on reclaiming the main building, its two wings, and the powerhouse. The $160 million restoration was one of the largest efforts ever completed in the United States. On the following pages this architectural tour documents the restoration process that began in 1982 and was completed for Ellis Island's reopening in 1990.

The registry room, as viewed from the west balcony, looked essentially like this to the renovation architectural team. Note ▶ that the floor's Ludowici tile is patterned after the Guastavino-tiled ceiling vault. The flooring's red quarry tile was remarkably clean, thanks to the National Park Service, which maintained it. However, looks can be deceptive. This room was not what early immigrants saw. Later-era water closets encroached on the far end; a modern stairway, added during the Coast Guard occupation in World War II, broke through the balcony rail. Expert eyes saw, documented, and dated the temporary partitions and light fixtures under the balconies as later additions. Early photographs also were consulted to confirm the later-period intrusions. The brass and glass chandeliers were removed temporarily, so that the restoration work would not harm them. A disturbing amount of water damage was visible at the base of the ceiling vault (far left). This damage suggested the subroof was rotting. This photo now hangs as a mural on permanent display in the Ellis Island Immigration Museum and in the Nation of Nations exhibit at the Smithsonian Institution in Washington, D.C. (Photo by Wilton S. Tifft)

The Great Hall was filled with scaffolding used by engineers and workmen repairing the interlocked dovetailed tiles. Rising like a tree with its branches nearly touching all surfaces of the vaulted ceiling, the scaffolding enabled workers to touch and test each of the 28,282 ceiling tiles. Only after such a close inspection could the tiles that needed repair or replacement be identified. The restoration team's operating philosophy was "never replace if repair is possible." (Photo by Wilton S. Tifft)

Once the magnificent Guastavino vaulted ceiling was cleaned and restored, pearlescent light again filtered down on the restoration team. All around the walls, however, decaying soft plaster and terra-cotta tiles were pulling away. Beneath the water damage, extensive wall damage and corrosion of the supporting steel were uncovered. Brick had been removed to reveal the slender steel column at left, which was repaired.

The chandeliers (two had been restored, the third is a reproduction) are shown boxed protectively in the wooden crates at the center of this picture.

Wooden handrails were padded so that they would not be damaged by the paint removal process. Old paint had to be sandblasted away from the ironwork and chemically removed from wall plaster and tiles. Before the cleaning, however, conservators removed paint and material samples from scores of locations throughout the room. These samples went through microscopic and laboratory examinations so that their original composition could be determined.

At intersections where later-era partitions were removed, the exposed walls revealed the registry room's many ornamental paint finishes, including black and a very dark green. The renovation re-created the color scheme used in the redecoration following the Black Tom explosion in 1916. (Photo by Wilton S. Tifft)

A simple scaffold was used to access plaster window surrounds and cornice work. Areas along the balcony where the Caen stone, an imitation limestone, had been lost or damaged beyond repair were built up. Eroded walls were filled in with replacement terra-cotta block, and steel armatures for plasterwork were reshaped. Notice that the damaged column on the far left has been repaired and rebricked and the later-period stairway is gone.

The building's old steam radiators were lined up along the floor after pressure testing and painting. Most of the original radiators passed the pressure testing. Banana-oil paints that were used in the 1890s to enliven otherwise dull-appearing radiators were reemployed on these brightly painted radiators.

A wooden barricade at the far end of the registry room floor is actually a safety rail around a newly cut stairway opening from the baggage room below. (Photo by Wilton S. Tifft)

In the late afternoon, as the sun begins to set and the lights are turned on, the fully restored Great Hall seems to glow. ▶
(Photo by Wilton S. Tifft)

A plaster craftsman just to the left of center works at his bench with an artisan's commitment to quality. Research identified the original plaster mixes, which were painstakingly duplicated to restore the original appearance and acoustics of the registry room. (Radiators not yet relocated were covered to protect them from the splatter of wet white plaster.)

All necessary electrical and mechanical work was roughed in. New duct openings can be seen over the balcony doors. They had been coordinated carefully to fall within the original stone pattern.

Paint research had rediscovered the precise shade of cream for the lower elements, but months of finishing work remained. The floor needed to be patched, chandeliers rehung, and hundreds of other cosmetic touch-ups were needed to complete the restoration. (Photo by Wilton S. Tifft)

Appended to the main building's northern side in 1904, the railroad ticket office served as the departure point for approximately two-thirds of the immigrants passing through Ellis Island. Those heading beyond New York City often lingered here, viewing the panorama of the New York skyline, the Hudson River, and the Central New Jersey Terminal. Historic photos like this one show the original ceiling, but after it collapsed (around 1913), exposing the original trusses and skylights, the ceiling was never replaced. (Photo courtesy of the New York Public Library)

▲ *Registry room benches had found their way here, and the floor was littered with debris. The steel, clay tiles, and floor in the room were examined carefully. The skylights leaked, but plaster and paint conditions suggested only mild deterioration. The pendant light fixtures along with a "modern" paint job were replaced with accurate restorations for the 1918–1924 period. (Photo by Wilton S. Tifft)*

The roof structure was repaired or replaced to protect the room. Skylights were repaired, raised, and redetailed. Window grating (left foreground) from Ellis Island's detention days was removed, and radiators were pulled for pressure testing.

  New fire protection sprinklers, along with mechanical and electrical work, were installed. However, the original ceiling was not replaced because it was already gone by 1918. The refurbished room houses exhibits on American and world immigration patterns. (Photo by Wilton S. Tifft)

This room in the west wing of the main building's second floor was either used for processing immigrants with special problems or for hearings. The plaster (left) suffered its worst deterioration near the exterior wall. The desks, papers, bench, and other artifacts left behind by the U.S. government became part of the museum's collection. This photo now hangs as a mural on permanent display in the Ellis Island Immigration Museum. (Photo by Wilton S. Tifft)

An early, though not original, doorway was discovered leading into the next processing room. A close inspection showed that the wooden moldings had been nailed over several coats of base paint. When the moldings were removed, they revealed twelve feet of men's names penciled on the bare plaster. The names are preserved for future generations in the museum's collection. (Photo by Wilton S. Tifft)

An air duct was installed in the window opening, but fortunately the original window was found. The flooring, often badly deteriorated, was removed and a concrete leveling slab poured to prepare for a new floor. (Photo by Wilton S. Tifft)

Much of the dead plaster was removed, the arched opening and column were reblocked, and electrical and drain lines were cut into place. Wooden subflooring had been installed over the concrete. (Photo by Wilton S. Tifft)

Restoration completed, from the shine on the polished wooden floor to the reproduction light fixtures and authentic cream-colored paint on the walls, the room was ready for installation of museum exhibits. (Photo by Wilton S. Tifft)

NINE

New Beginnings

The Statue of Liberty is possibly the best-known monument to freedom in the world. Yet within the glow of her torch lies another American symbol—Ellis Island, the best-known emblem of hope in America.

In May 1965 President Lyndon B. Johnson recognized the significance of both the Statue of Liberty and Ellis Island as inseparably intertwined American monuments when he signed a proclamation making the federal immigration station part of the Statue of Liberty National Monument. He reaffirmed this relationship in a visit to the monument the same year, noting, "America has flourished because it was fed from . . . so many cultures, traditions, and people."

Bearing testimony to this vision of our country, Ellis Island reopened its doors in the fall of 1990 after a seven-year, $160 million restoration paid for by the American people.

As the first visitors disembarked, Ellis Island's main building once again welcomed people beneath its canopied walkway. But this time no one was turned away. The footsteps were not those of immigrants but of their children and their children's children, who came in celebration of their ancestors' fortitude and determination to forge a better life.

The centerpiece of the restoration effort is the magnificent hundred-thousand-square-foot Ellis Island Immigration Museum located in the main building. Spread throughout all three levels of the structure, the museum is one of New York's largest cultural and educational institutions, attracting almost two million visitors each year.

The museum's exhibits have been designed to work within the existing building configuration. Many of the rooms are restored, while others have been adapted or altered to make better use of the interior space.

Wherever visitors go, they encounter the immigrants—see their faces, hear their voices, read their words. "More than anything else," says a park service official, "the exhibits give voice to the newcomers themselves. Each story is unique, but together they speak to the commonalities of the immigration experience."

The "Peopling of America" display, located in the old railroad ticket office on the first floor, graphically interprets the statistics of American immigration so that major trends may be understood.

"Through America's Gate," on the second floor of the west wing, uses photographs, artifacts, personal papers, and oral histories to reveal step by step what most new arrivals experienced on Ellis Island.

On the second floor of the east wing, "Peak Immigration Years: 1880–1924" explores immigration to the United States during that period, regardless of the port of entry. Displays portray the immigrant experience, from leaving the homeland to becoming an American citizen.

The third floor of the east wing houses the "Ellis Island Chronicles," an exhibit which traces the history of Ellis Island from its oyster-bed beginnings to the present; "Treasures From Home," a display built around hundreds of artifacts brought to America by immigrants; and "Silent Voices," a gallery that focuses on Ellis Island's years of abandonment and its restoration.

An immigration research library and an oral history center occupy the third floor of the west wing. The center contains approximately six hundred interviews recounting the experiences of immigrants and former Ellis Island employees during the island's operating years between 1892 and 1954. The center

Bathed in early morning light, this angelic stone face on the keystone of the main entrance placidly gazes down on visitors to the Ellis Island Immigration Museum just as it once gazed down on each of the 12 million immigrants who passed through this portal. (Photo by Wilton S. Tifft)

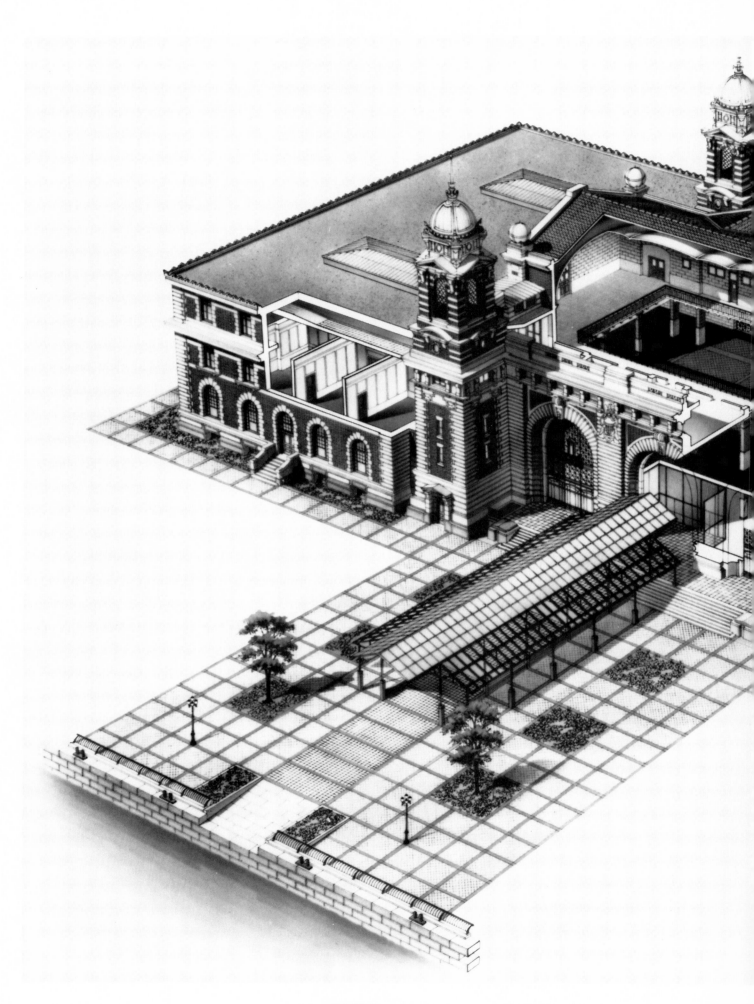

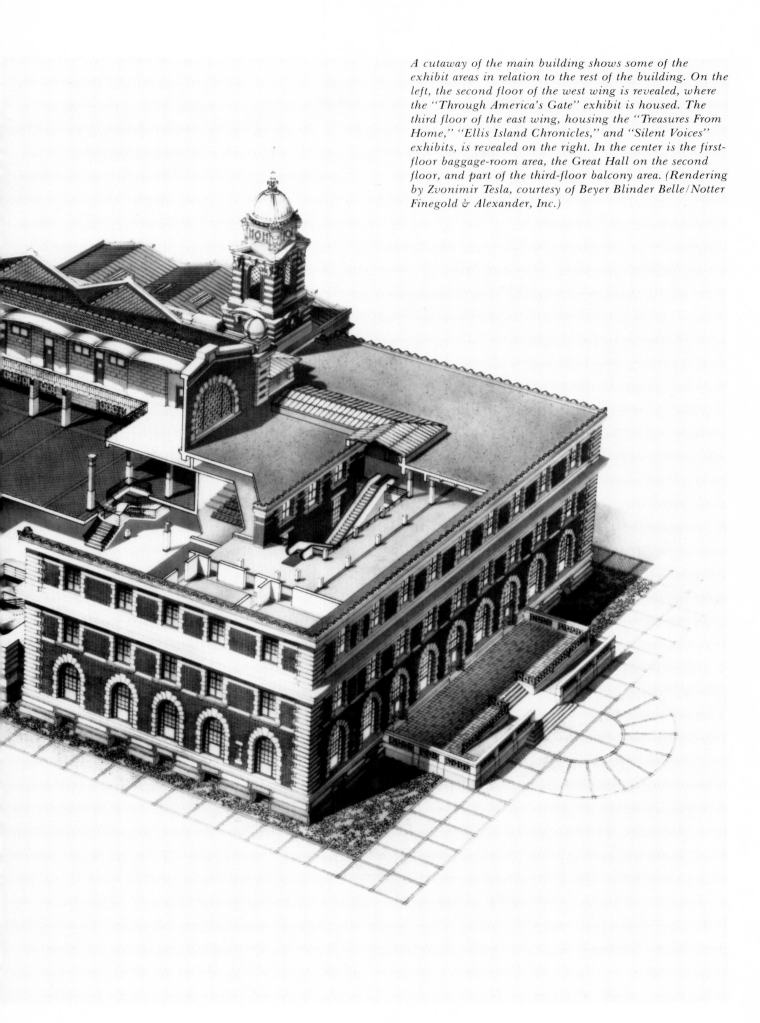

A cutaway of the main building shows some of the exhibit areas in relation to the rest of the building. On the left, the second floor of the west wing is revealed, where the "Through America's Gate" exhibit is housed. The third floor of the east wing, housing the "Treasures From Home," "Ellis Island Chronicles," and "Silent Voices" exhibits, is revealed on the right. In the center is the first-floor baggage-room area, the Great Hall on the second floor, and part of the third-floor balcony area. (Rendering by Zvonimir Tesla, courtesy of Beyer Blinder Belle/Notter Finegold & Alexander, Inc.)

The "Peopling of America" exhibit presents immigration statistics in dramatic multimedia displays. This is an early conceptual drawing of part of the exhibit. (Drawing courtesy of the U.S. Department of the Interior, National Park Service)

also includes a recording studio so that former immigrants and former employees visiting the museum can add their experiences to the collection.

To celebrate thousands of immigrants who risked everything to come to America, a special memorial—The American Immigrant Wall of Honor—has been built along the seawall east of the main building. Completed in 1990, the monument contains almost two hundred thousand names of immigrants enrolled by families and friends who donated a minimum of $100 to help restore Ellis Island. The names are representative of newcomers from all seven continents and date as far back as the Pilgrims. Among the more noted listings are John Washington, great-grandfather of the first president; Paul Revere's father, Paul Revoire; Myles Standish; Priscilla Alden; the eight great-grandparents of John F. Kennedy; John Jacob

Astor; Al Jolson; Oscar Hammerstein I; and Frances Cabrini, the first American saint. All registered names, along with their country of origin and the name of the donor, are available to museum visitors on a computer register.

Restored, Ellis Island is a tribute to those early newcomers who believed in the Land of Opportunity. Like life itself, the former immigration station, now transformed into a national museum, is a complex study of contrasts—the dark shadows of desperation, pain, and rejection accent the bright lights of love, hope, and rebirth.

The Statue of Liberty beckoned the many yearning for freedom. Ellis Island processed the many into one indivisible nation. Together Lady Liberty and Ellis Island epitomize the motto of the United States of America: *e pluribus unum*, "From Many, One."

An artist's early sketch shows how the "Peopling of America" exhibit will utilize the space in the old railroad ticket office. Through graphs, maps, and interactive displays, this exhibit is designed to help visitors understand the major trends in immigration to America. (Drawing courtesy of the U.S. Department of the Interior, National Park Service)

This early conceptual drawing of the "Through America's Gate" exhibit depicts how visitors can use an interactive console and examine artifacts to learn more about the medical exam and the hospital facilities. (Drawing courtesy of the U.S. Department of the Interior, National Park Service)

"Through America's Gate" will take the visitor step by step through the immigration process on Ellis Island. An artist's sketch suggests how the various world currencies that were exchanged for U.S. dollars on the island might be displayed. (Drawing courtesy of the U.S. Department of the Interior, National Park Service)

The displays in the "Peak Immigration Years: 1880–1924" portray the immigrant experience, from leaving the homeland to becoming a U.S. citizen. This early model shows how a display of immigrant occupations might be set up. (Illustration courtesy of the U.S. Department of the Interior, National Park Service)

In another model, visitors learn more about the voyage to America through an interactive multimedia display. (Illustration courtesy of the U.S. Department of the Interior, National Park Service)

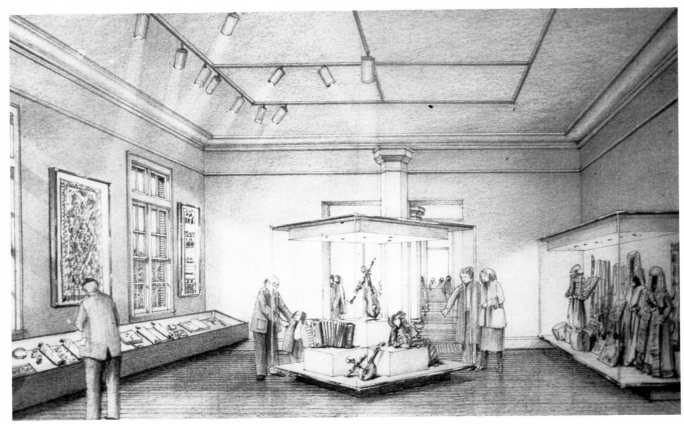

The "Treasures From Home" exhibit displays thousands of artifacts brought to America by immigrants. This is an early conceptual drawing of the exhibit. (Drawing courtesy of the U.S. Department of the Interior, National Park Service)

The registry room or Great Hall, on the second floor of the main building, was completely restored to the 1918–1924 period. This artist's sketch shows a ranger answering questions while some visitors pause to rest on the restored benches. (Drawing courtesy of the U.S. Department of the Interior, National Park Service)

Visitors to the museum pass through the main entrance into the old baggage-room area on the first floor. (Drawing courtesy of the U.S. Department of the Interior, National Park Service)

Completed in 1990, The American Immigrant Wall of Honor contains almost two hundred thousand names. Depicted here in an early conceptual drawing, the waist-high wall runs along the island's eastern seawall. (Illustration courtesy of the Statue of Liberty–Ellis Island Foundation)

Author's Note

My fascination with Ellis Island began in early 1968. Resting serenely beside the Statue of Liberty sat an abandoned yet dignified island with its decaying turn-of-the-century buildings. These deserted and deteriorating brick-and-limestone buildings, which once ushered twelve million immigrants into the New World, presented an intriguing foreground to the surrounding Manhattan, New Jersey, and Liberty Island cityscapes.

I was curious about this desolate and overgrown island with its once-magnificent buildings. So I obtained permission from the National Park Service to visit and photograph Ellis Island.

From my first visit I was drawn to learn more of the island's checkered past and to speculate on its then-uncertain future. Wandering through rooms strewn with furniture, clothes, and eating utensils was an experience I will never forget. Except for a fine frosting of plaster dust and peeling ceilings and walls, these rooms looked as if their occupants had planned to return and pick up where they had stopped in 1954, when Ellis Island quietly closed its doors.

There was no heat or electricity on the island to chase away the chill of wintry days or water to cool a parched summer throat. Surprisingly, however, there was one functional telephone in the basement, which the National Park Service ranger pointed out to me on my first visit.

The grounds surrounding the buildings were heavily overgrown with trees, vines, and brambles of every description. There was a wonderful collection of fruit trees from which I enjoyed many apples, pears, and peaches over the years, and I found a wide

Author Wilton S. Tifft poses with his cameras on the balcony overlooking the renovated and restored Great Hall. (Photo by Brian Feeney)

assortment of berries to augment the lunches I brought.

One winter a pair of snowy owls were using the east balcony of the registry room as their nesting site. They entered and exited the building through an open window, and as I would enter the registry room I could hear their rustling and then see these magnificent birds take flight. In the eerie silence they would circle the upper reaches of the domed room on whispering wings and then quietly exit through the open arched window, not to return until I left.

I cannot say that I saw or met any ghosts or apparitions during my more than twenty years photographing Ellis Island. However, from my first visit I did experience a very strong spiritual presence that I still feel today. It was as if Ellis Island's hopes and tears were with me, guiding my eyes to see this deserted federal immigration station as an old and waning friend. I do feel that Ellis Island is my friend; for having been granted this privilege, I am both honored and grateful.

During the late 1960s and early 1970s I had several shows featuring my Ellis Island photographs. My work was honored with the New York Art Directors Club Award and the Publication Designers Award. In 1971 my first book, *Ellis Island*, was published by W. W. Norton. Since America's Bicentennial in 1976 my photograph of the registry room has been displayed as a wall mural in the "Nation of Nations" exhibit at the Smithsonian Institution's National Museum of American History in Washington, D.C.

Even now, after more than two decades of documenting Ellis Island, I still feel the magic of that dear friend, who finally is benefiting from a well-deserved and long-awaited renovation and restoration.

I continued to photograph the progress of the restoration with special attention to several areas that I first captured on film in the 1960s. (Six of my photographs, done as Carbro prints by R. L. McCowan

Diana Pardue is the curator of the Ellis Island Immigration Museum for the National Park Service. (Photo by Wilton S. Tifft)

Kevin C. Buckley, Superintendent of the Statue of Liberty National Monument, stopped for a portrait on Ellis Island. Behind him is the main building. (Photo by Wilton S. Tifft)

Dwarfed by the dimensions of the registry room but not by the task, some of the men who directed this historic project pause during an inspection tour for a picture. From left to right: Kevin C. Buckley; Herbert S. Cables, Jr., Deputy Director of the National Park Service; Vincent Benic, Senior Project Inspector, Beyer Blinder Belle; Bruce Heyl, Project Manager, Beyer Blinder Belle; John Belle, Partner-in-charge, Beyer Blinder Belle; James Rhodes, Project Manager, Beyer Blinder Belle; Michael Adlerstein, Project Director, Statue of Liberty–Ellis Island, National Park Service; and Charles Clapper, Assistant Regional Director, North Atlantic Region, National Park Service. (Photo by Wilton S. Tifft)

The staff of the preservation architectural firm, Beyer Blinder Belle/Notter Finegold & Alexander, gathered in the Great Hall for this portrait. From left to right: Don Porter, Don Fiorino, James Rhodes, Frank Powell, Elmer Horvath, Ilija Mosscrop, Maxinne Leighton, Howard Rosenfield, Bonnie Sevy, Bruce Heyl, Marc Wilkins, Nan Gutterman, Sherman Morss, Richard Curran, Allan Swerdlowe, Gretchen Shimanek, Richard Franko, Ralph Carmosino, Tim Allanbrook, Judith Angel, Jacob Majnemer, Elizabeth Ballantine, Blesilda Arceo, Page Ayres, Nancy Lenz, Tony Chavarria, Steve Roth, Vincent Benic. (Photo by Wilton S. Tifft)

Coordinating the design, selection, assembly, and construction of the museum exhibits was the responsibility of the Ellis Island Immigration Museum Project Team from the Harpers Ferry (VA) office of the National Park Service. They are (from left to right): Michael P. Paskowsky, Interpretive Planner; Alan Levitan, Conservation Coordinator; Grant Cadwallader, Exhibit Production Consultant; Thomas P. K. Radford, A.V. Production Officer; Gary G. Roth, Project Manager; and Toby Raphael, Conservation Coordinator. (Photo by Wilton S. Tifft)

of St. Louis, are exhibited as wall murals in the island's museum complex.) Using the same cameras and lenses, I photographed these sites during the reconstruction to illustrate Ellis Island's metamorphosis from ruin and desolation to the grandeur of the authentically restored buildings today. The transformation has been like that of a butterfly that emerges from its cocoon to display its splendor.

Much assistance was provided by John Belle and Jim Rhodes at Beyer Blinder Belle/Notter Finegold & Alexander, the architectural joint venture on the restoration and renovation. National Park Service historical architects Michael Adlerstein and Peter F. Dessauer also enlarged my understanding of the hundreds of steps involved in the reconstruction and restoration project.

My continued access to Ellis Island was assured by the National Park Service, from Chief Ranger W. Pingree Crawford in the 1960s through Superintendent Kevin Buckley, who is currently in charge of Ellis Island.

The cameras used to record Ellis Island over the years are 35mm Leica M-series rangefinders. All of my prints in this book are done on Ilford Galeria paper, and my current choices of film are Ilford HP5 and FP4.

From the photography to a book is a long and complicated process, and I am grateful for the assistance, cooperation, and support of a great many people in this endeavor. If I have inadvertently forgotten anyone, I apologize.

Dr. Richard G. Frederick of the University of Pittsburgh at Bradford was instrumental in researching and preparing the text. Linda Bredengerd of the University of Pittsburgh Library, assisted in obtaining documents and research materials. Myra Vanderpool Gormley kindly gave permission to use portions of her articles.

For their willingness to answer questions and provide information or materials, I'd like to thank Ed Kallop, Paul Kinney, Steve Lewis, Diana Pardue, and Deputy Director Herbert Cables, Jr., at the National

The National Park Service staff of the Statue of Liberty/Ellis Island National Monument take a moment out of their busy schedules for a picture. From left to right: Mike Ryan, Mike Kusch, Brian Feeney, Peter Dessauer, Cathleen Hurst, Theresa Stoia, Felice Ciccione, Denise Chicketano, Ray Owens, Jeff Dosik, Joe Wong, Kim Porter, Ken Glasgow, Donald Grace, and Joanne Timmins. (Photo by Wilton S. Tifft)

Park Service; Barbara Grazzini, Ziva Bender, Gary Kelly, and Peg Zitco at the Statue of Liberty–Ellis Island Foundation; Debra Joester at Hamilton Projects, Inc.; Phyllis Montgomery and Fred Wasserman at Metaform/Rathe/D&P; Ronnie Greico at Leica U.S.A.; Richard Schleuning, Laurie Dicara, and Berry Sinclair at Ilford Photo Corporation; Bonnie Yochelson, Curator of Prints and Photographs at the Museum of the City of New York; Bernard F. Reilly, Head Curator, the Library of Congress; the National Archives; the New York Public Library; the YIVO Institute for Jewish Research; the University of Michigan (Bentley Library); the University of Wisconsin; the Minnesota Historical Society; and B'nai B'rith.

I extend my deepest appreciation and gratitude to my agent, Julian Bach; my publisher, Harvey Plotnick; and "Editor Supreme" Bernard Shir-Cliff as well as to the editorial and design team at Contemporary Books that has shared my enthusiasm for this project: J. D. Fairbanks, Tonia Payne, Christine Benton, Rita Tatum, Bill Ewing, Georgene Sainati, Katherine Willhoite, Julia Walski, Christine Albritton, and Mary Eley.

Other individuals who have given me much sup-port and encouragement over the years and deserve mention are Brian Feeney from the National Park Service, who took the author's photograph for me, Shirley C. Burden, Oliver Jensen, Helen Wright, Emmy and Paulus Leeser, Arnold Newman, Jacob Deschin, Charlie Reynolds, Sam Holmes, Merle Pollack, Steve Woodcheck and the crew at Lehrer McGovern Bovis, Spiros Polemis at Helicon Press, Tom Dunne, Marcel Lissek, Arthur Voyer, Spiros Cotakis, "Barb" Costanzo, Anika-Jans, Sleu, and Chloe.

I am relieved that Ellis Island has been and continues to be preserved in an appropriate manner. The restoration and reconstruction have removed the debris and decay, allowing a pristine facility to emerge in radiant beauty. However, I have felt a pang of regret as the footprints of the immigrants were swept away. I now see my old friend in a "new suit of clothes," knowing that the renovation has been necessary for this monument's survival. Otherwise there would be nothing but photographs to mark the immigrants' rites of passage.

I hope you come to love Ellis Island as I do.

—Wilton S. Tifft, April 1990

Directing the restoration work was the Ellis Island Project Team from the Denver Service Center of the National Park Service. They are (from left to right): William L. Wittmer, Chief of Planning, TEA/DSC/NPS; Peter Dessauer, Project Supervisor, TEA/DSC/NPS; Donald A. Falvey, Chief of Team East, DSC/NPS; Richard E. Wells, Project Director, TEA/DSC/NPS; and Robert S. Budz, Chief of Design, TEA/DSC/NPS. (Photo by Wilton S. Tifft)

The group that spearheaded the fund-raising for the restoration of Ellis Island was the Statue of Liberty–Ellis Island Foundation. The staff gathered in the registry room for a group photo: (from left to right, front row) Ziva Benderly, Associate Director of Restoration and Preservation; Gary E. Kelley, Vice President and Controller; William F. May, Chairman and Chief Executive Officer; and Stephen A. Briganti, President and Chief Operating Officer; (from left to right, back row) Nick Cerulli, Peter B. Kaplan, Barbara Grazzini, Harriet Katz, Philip Cheng, Peter Zabriskie, Leslie Carter, Chris White, Shari Jakubowitz, Karl Anderson, Florence Kaplan, Peg Zitko, David Santana, Anna Maria Aniban, Sharyn McKenna, Bob Kerler, Maria Antenocruz, Connie Solomon, Jerrod Sanders, Diane Adams, Mark Honaker, Emily Lowe. (Photo by Wilton S. Tifft)

The museum exhibits were actually created by the staff of Metaform/Rathe/D&P pictured here: (from left to right) Mary-Angela Hardwick, Ray Short, Gina Russell, Barbara Gertzen, Phyllis Montgomery, Elizabeth Wilmerding, John Grady, Christina Trimble, Chris Farley, Tom Geismar, Ivan Chermayeff, Betsy Friedman, Fred Wasserman, Steve Bamonte, Robin Parkinson, Jack Masey, and Silvia Koner. (Photo by Wilton S. Tifft)

The contractor on this historic project was Lehrer McGovern Bovis, Inc. The staff is pictured here: (from left to right, front row) Thomas Peters, P. Philip Cannata, Ronald Miller, Patricia D'Agostino, Elizabeth A. O'Connor, Ana Cruzado, Steven Rich, John Englert, Haim Hershkovitz, Richard Nealy, Parviz Mehran, Stephen Woodcheke; (from left to right, back row) William Bessette, Daniel Cilla, Michael McCann, Paul Harris, Jerome Blakely, Kenneth S. Faulds, Thomas O'Connor, James Washington, Beth Leahy, Demetrius Samadjopoulis, Roy Pettyjohn, Donald Shortell, Margaret Van Voast, William Quiles, Kenneth Champion, Robert Pasqual. (Photo by Wilton S. Tifft)

© 1990 Wilton S. Tifft

A project of this size and scope is also labor intensive. Pictured at left is a representative group of the hundreds of construction workers needed to complete the project. Pictured above, these members of the Sheet Metal Workers' Union represent all the trade unions that participated. (Photos by Wilton S. Tifft)

Bibliography

BOOKS

Abbott, Edith. *Historical Aspects of the Immigration Problem: Select Documents*. Chicago: University of Chicago Press, 1926.

————. *Immigration: Select Documents and Case Records*. Chicago: University of Chicago Press, 1924.

Allen, Leslie. *Liberty: The Statue and the American Dream*. New York: Statue of Liberty–Ellis Island Foundation, Inc., 1985.

Benton, Barbara. *Ellis Island: A Pictorial History*. New York: Facts on File Publications, 1985.

Blegen, Theodore C., ed. *Land of Their Choice: The Immigrants Write Home*. Minneapolis: University of Minnesota Press, 1955.

Bliven, Bruce, Jr. *New York: A Bicentennial History*. New York: W. W. Norton & Company, Inc., 1981.

Brandenburg, Broughton. *Imported Americans: The Story of the Experiences of a Disguised American and His Wife Studying the Immigration Question*. New York: Frederick A. Stokes Company, 1904.

Charyn, Jerome. *Metropolis: New York as Myth, Marketplace, and Magical Land*. New York: Putnam Publishing Group, 1986.

Claghorn, Kate Holladay. *The Immigrant's Day in Court*. New York and London: Harper & Brothers Publishers, 1923.

Corsi, Edward. *In the Shadow of Liberty*. New York: Macmillan Company, 1935.

Cowen, Philip. *Memories of an American Jew*. New York: International Press, 1932.

Curran, Henry H. *Pillar to Post*. New York: Charles Scribner's Sons, 1941.

Fleming, Thomas. *New Jersey: A Bicentennial History*. New York: W. W. Norton & Company, Inc., 1977.

Goodwin, Maud Wilder. *Dutch and English on the Hudson*. New Haven: Yale University Press, 1919.

Heaps, Willard A. *The Story of Ellis Island*. New York: Seabury Press, 1967.

Higham, John. *Strangers in the Land: Patterns of American Nativism 1860–1925*. New York: Atheneum, 1973.

Howe, Frederic C. *The Confessions of a Reformer*. New York: Charles Scribner's Sons, 1925.

Kapp, Freidrich. *Immigration, and the Commissioners of Emigration of the State of New York*. New York: Nation Press, 1870.

Mardikian, George M. *Song of America*. New York: McGraw-Hill Book Company, Inc., 1956.

Morison, Elting E., ed. *The Letters of Theodore Roosevelt*. 8 vols. Cambridge: Harvard University Press, 1951–1954.

Novotny, Ann. *Strangers at the Door: Ellis Island, Castle Garden, and the Great Migration to America*. Riverside, Conn.: Chatham Press, Inc., 1971.

Pitkin, Thomas. *Keepers of the Gate: A History of Ellis Island*. New York: New York University Press, 1975.

Riis, Jacob. *The Battle with the Slum*. New York: Macmillan Company, 1902.

Ritchie, Robert C. *The Duke's Province: A Study of New York Politics and Society, 1664–1691*. Chapel Hill: University of North Carolina Press, 1977.

Steiner, Edward A. *On the Trail of the Immigrant*. New York: Fleming H. Revell Company, 1906.

Stevenson, Robert Louis. *The Amateur Emigrant: From the Clyde to Sandy Hook*. Chicago: Stone & Kimball, 1895.

Taylor, Philip. *The Distant Magnet: European Emigration to the U.S.A.* New York: Harper & Row, 1971.

West, Herbert Faulkner, ed. *The Autobiography of Robert Watchorn*. Oklahoma City: Robert Watchorn Charities, Ltd., 1958.

Wittke, Carl. *We Who Built America: The Saga of the Immigrant*. Cleveland: Press of Case Western Reserve University, 1964.

OTHER MATERIALS

Abbott, Ernest Hamlin. "America's Welcome to the Immigrant." *Outlook*, 72 (October 4, 1902), 256–64.

"The Bennet-Howe Controversy." *Outlook*, 113 (August 2, 1916), 763–64.

Durland, Kellogg. "Steerage Impositions." *Independent*, 61 (August 30, 1906), 499–504.

"For a Better Ellis Island." *Outlook*, 107 (October 21, 1914), 402–3.

Foster, Milton H. "A General Hospital for all Nations." *Survey*, 33 (February 27, 1915), 588–90.

Gratz, Roberta Brandes, and Eric Fettmann. "The Battle for Ellis Island." *Nation*, 241 (November 30, 1985), 579–82.

————. "The Selling of Miss Liberty." *Nation*, 241 (November 9, 1985), 465–76.

Great Britain, Foreign Office. "Despatch from H.M. Ambassador at Washington reporting on Conditions at Ellis Island Immigration Station." London: H.M. Stationery Office, 1923.

Harrison, Shelby M. "The Anomalous Quarantine Situation in New York Bay." *Survey*, 27 (January 27, 1912), 1640-43.

MacBrayne, Lewis E. "The Judgment of the Steerage." *Harper's Monthly Magazine*, 117 (September 1908), 489-99.

McLaughlin, Dr. Allan. "How Immigrants Are Inspected." *Popular Science Monthly*, 66 (February 1905), 357-61.

"The New Ellis Island: An Interview with Dr. Frederic C. Howe, Commissioner of Immigration at Ellis Island." *The Immigrants in America Review*, 1 (June 1915), 10-12.

New York Times, various dates, 1890-1988.

Ogg, Frederic Austin. "A New Plan for Immigrant Inspection." *Outlook*, 83 (May 5, 1906), 33-36.

Ralph, Julian. "Landing the Immigrant." *Harper's Weekly*, 35 (October 24, 1891), 821-24.

Rhodes, Benjamin D. "A Modern 'Black Hole of Calcutta'? The Anglo-American Controversy over Ellis Island, 1921-1924." *New York History*, 66 (July 1985), 228-48.

Riis, Jacob A. "In the Gateway of Nations." *Century*, 65 (March 1903), 674-82.

Salmon, Thomas M., M.D. "Federal Quarantine at New York." *Survey*, 30 (April 26, 1913), 139-40.

Sargent, Frank P. "The Need of Closer Inspection and Greater Restriction of Immigrants." *Century*, 67 (January 1904), 470-73.

Shaler, Nathaniel S. "European Peasants as Immigrants." *Atlantic Monthly*, 71 (May 1893), 646-55.

Sherwood, Herbert Francis. "The Silent Keeper of the Gate." *Outlook*, 89 (June 6, 1908), 289-96.

Sprague, E. K., M.D. "Medical Inspection of Immigrants." *Survey*, 30 (June 21, 1913), 420-22.

————. "Mental Examination of Immigrants." *Survey*, 31 (January 17, 1914), 466-68.

Unrau, Harlan D. "Historic Resource Study (Historical Component): Ellis Island." 3 vols. U.S. Department of the Interior/National Park Service, 1984.

Watchorn, Robert. "The Gateway of the Nation." *Outlook*, 87 (December 28, 1907), 897-912.

Whitmarsh, H. Phelps. "The Steerage of To-Day. A Personal Experience." *Century*, 55 (February 1898), 528-43.

Williams, L. L. "A Leak in Quarantine: Stricter Measures Needed on Immigrant Ships." *Survey*, 33 (December 12, 1914), 291-92.

Index

Index of Photographers,
Illustrators, and Other Sources